# *Structuralism: an introduction*

# *Structuralism:*
## *an introduction*

WOLFSON COLLEGE LECTURES 1972

EDITED BY
DAVID ROBEY

CLARENDON PRESS · OXFORD
1973

*Oxford University Press, Ely House, London W.1*

GLASGOW NEW YORK TORONTO MELBOURNE WELLINGTON
CAPE TOWN IBADAN NAIROBI DAR ES SALAAM LUSAKA ADDIS ABABA
DELHI CALCUTTA MADRAS KARACHI LAHORE DACCA
KUALA LUMPUR SINGAPORE HONG KONG TOKYO



PRINTED IN GREAT BRITAIN BY
WILLIAM CLOWES & SONS, LIMITED
LONDON, BECCLES AND COLCHESTER

# *Preface*

THE chapters contained in this volume originally constituted the 1972 Wolfson College Lectures on the subject of Structuralism. They have undergone varying degrees of rewriting. In particular Jonathan Culler's and John Mepham's contributions were specially composed for the book, on the basis of a seminar which they gave together in the series; Tzvetan Todorov's study has been published elsewhere in French. The editor's warm thanks go to the Trustees, President, and Fellows of Wolfson College for financing the lectures, to Michael Argyle as co-organizer of them, to Mrs. Beryl Schweder for considerable administrative and secretarial help, and to Mrs. Elizabeth Scaramanga and Miss Serena Denholm-Young for the difficult job of retyping some of the contributions.

DAVID ROBEY

*Oxford*, 24 October 1972

# *Contents*

# *Introduction*

DAVID ROBEY

IN linguistics, the starting-point of this series of lectures, Structuralism has its formal beginnings in the *Thèses* presented collectively by the members of the Prague Linguistic Circle to the First International Congress of Slavic Philologists held in Prague in 1929.[1] A radically innovatory programme for the theory and methodology of linguistic study, the *Thèses* introduced the notion of *structure* as the key term in a polemic against the traditional methods of the discipline, over-concerned, in their authors' view, with problems of linguistic origin, and limited to the analysis of isolated facts. Under the influence of Saussure and the Russian linguist Baudouin de Courtenay, the authors of the *Thèses* proposed language as a functional *system*, to be understood in the light of its *aim* (that of communication). *Structure*, in the *Thèses*, is the structure of the system, the manner in which the individual elements of a particular language are arranged for this purpose in relations of mutual dependence. Since this differs from one language to another, it follows that the separate components of a system can only be understood in the light of the system as a whole, and therefore that the primary object of linguistic study must be the structure of the system itself rather than the individual linguistic fact. It is in this sense that the method of modern linguistics should be, as the *Thèses* suggest, *structural*; and, with slight variations, this has continued to be the basis of the notion of structural linguistics, at least in Europe, up to the present day.

This gives us the starting-point for one possible definition of Structural*ism*: as that approach—to any subject—which has as its object, in the words of the *Thèses*, the 'laws of solidarity', the 'reciprocal relations' of the different facts under observation, rather than considering these facts in isolation. It is in this sense that the word is used by Trubetzkoy, one of the leading members of the Prague circle, in an article of 1933: 'The age in which we live is characterized', he wrote, 'by the tendency of all scientific disciplines to replace atomism with structuralism, and individualism with universalism.'[2] This understanding of Structuralism as an interdisciplinary trend—common, in Trubetzkoy's view, to such diverse subjects as physics, chemistry, biology, psychology, and economics—was taken up most notably by Cassirer and Piaget. 'Structuralism', Cassirer wrote in 1945, 'is no isolated phenomenon; it is, rather, the expression of a general tendency of thought that, in these last decades, has become more and more prominent in almost all fields of scientific research.'[3] More recently, and with greater precision, Piaget has defined Structuralism as a method of inquiry based on the concepts of totality, self-regulation, and transformation, common not only to anthropology and linguistics, but to mathematics, physics, biology, psychology, and philosophy as well.[4]

But to avoid confusion it is important to distinguish between this meaning of Structuralism and another, narrower acceptation of the term. Structuralism in this second sense represents a much more distinctive body of thought which, though assuming the principles of Structuralism in my first definition, derives specifically from the Structuralist theories that have been elaborated in the field of linguistics. Inspired by a famous passage in Saussure's *Cours de linguistique générale*, and founded in the anthropology of Lévi-Strauss, this new science (as it claims to be) has grown out of the supposition that the theories and methods of structural linguistics are directly or indirectly applicable to the analysis of all aspects of human culture, in so far as all of these, like language, may be interpreted as systems of signs. Structuralism in this sense is more or less coterminous, as Jonathan Culler points out, with *semiology* or *semiotics*, the science of signs, as Saussure says, 'au sein de la vie sociale'. It is principally, though perforce not exclusively, on this understanding of the term that the following essays are based.

Evidently as an introduction to this topic the lecture-series form has its defects; but, it is hoped, the inherent interest of such a group of contributions will compensate for the inevitable inadequacies of the method of exposition. The chapters that follow will at all events attempt to give a broad account of the theoretical foundations of the subject and also of its general scope. So after John Lyons's presentation of Structuralism in linguistics, Jonathan Culler discusses the general question of the applicability of linguistic methods of analysis to other, non-linguistic fields of research. Edmund Leach gives an outline of structural anthropology, and in particular of the work of Lévi-Strauss, the model for all subsequent attempts at the extension of linguistic theory beyond the borders of its own discipline. Umberto Eco examines some of the problems involved in the constitution of semiotics (or semiology) as an independent discipline, and in so doing raises a number of issues concerning the application of structuralist methods of analysis to social phenomena in general.

This completes the exposition of the topic. Leaving to specialist publications the task of offering further examples of structuralist methods of analysis, it seemed better to devote the remaining contributions to a general discussion of some of the broader issues raised by structuralist theory, and to an illustration of its use in the sphere of literary criticism. Robin Gandy therefore deals with the question of structure in mathematics, the structuralist science (in my first definition) *par exellence*, with a view to clarifying the use of this notion in its application to other fields. John Mepham takes up the issue of the significance of Structuralism in the light of the general theory of science, and in relation to the ontology of the subject. Finally there is Tzvetan Todorov's chapter on the structural analysis of literature, illustrated in a study of the tales of Henry James. His contribution, and particularly his prefatory remarks, need to be read with care. Structuralism in literary theory (according to my *second* definition of the term) is not concerned with the interpretation of individual works. It is a general science, the object of which is the system or series of systems of conventions and procedures (in the last analysis, signs) which constitute the distinctive features of literature as a whole. Tzvetan Todorov's study is therefore offered as an example of the use which may be made of structuralist tools, in the analysis of style, narrative technique, plot structures, etc., by an essentially independent activity of interpretation. Structuralism may be the framework within which the interpretation occurs, but it is separate from the interpretation itself. However, Todorov's interpretation of James *is* structuralist in my *first* sense of the term, since its purpose is also to present James's stories as unified *structures*, through an examination of the interrelations of the different levels of each work.

At a time when the re-edition of a recent work on Structuralism (in my second sense) has suggested that the theory has already been superseded,[5] it may seem strange that a general introduction to the subject should be felt to be necessary. But if the discussion on Structuralism has made rapid (perhaps too rapid) progress in the last few years, especially in France, its initial principles have not yet been shown to be invalid, nor do they deserve the neglect which, no doubt on account of a traditional suspicion of theory, they have continued to suffer in this country. On the other hand it is important that Structuralism should not be regarded as in any sense a finished body of doctrine. Its conceptual apparatus may well require a considerable amount of adjustment, and certain important issues—notably those of the ontological status of structures, and of the exact nature of the relationship with linguistics—are still very much a subject of discussion, as the contributions which follow will show. I would propose, then, that it is on the basis of the potential which the fruitfulness of its methods suggests that Structuralism should be judged; it offers itself as an unusually promising way of considering social and cultural phenomena, and not yet, at least—though no doubt some of its exponents would disagree with this—as a definitive theory of culture and society.

For further bibliographical information I refer the reader to two relatively recent works on Structuralism: *The Structuralist Controversy*, edited by Richard Macksey and Eugenio Donato (The Johns Hopkins Press, Baltimore, Md., and London, 1972); *Structuralism: A Reader*, edited and introduced by Michael Lane (Jonathan Cape, London, 1970).

NOTES

1. *Travaux du Cercle Linguistique de Prague*, i (1929), 5–29; cf. E. Benveniste, '"Structure" en linguistique', in *Sens et usages du terme 'structure' dans les sciences humaines et sociales*, ed. R. Bastide (Mouton, The Hague, 1962), pp. 32–8.
2. N. Trubetzkoy, 'La Phonologie actuelle', *Journal de Psychologie*, xxx (1933), 246.
3. E. Cassirer, 'Structuralism in Modern Linguistics', *Word*, i (1945), 120.
4. Jean Piaget, *Le Structuralisme* (P.U.F., Paris, 1968).
5. *The Structuralist Controversy* (cited above), pp. ix ff.

# 1 *Structuralism and Linguistics*

JOHN LYONS

IN preparing my contribution to the present series of lectures on structuralism I have assumed that there will be some members of the audience for whom the so-called structural approach to the study of language is relatively unfamiliar. I shall therefore concentrate upon giving a straightforward exposition of the principal structuralist theses in linguistics; and I shall try to make my observations as comprehensible and self-contained as possible. The inevitable consequence of adopting this view of the subject is that I shall, for most of the time at least, be merely rehearsing what are for many members of the audience rather hackneyed points and illustrating them with all too familiar examples. Since my lecture comes first in the series, I see it as an important part of my task to introduce and explain as clearly as I can a number of general concepts, including the notion of 'structure' itself, which other contributors will be drawing upon and applying within their various disciplines in subsequent lectures.

Before moving into the subject proper, I must make one terminological caveat. The expression 'structuralism' has acquired two distinct senses in current linguistic discussion. In one of its senses, it refers to the views and methodology of the dominant school of American linguistics in the 1940s and 1950s: the so-called post-Bloomfieldian school, which culminated in Zellig Harris's, *Methods in Structual Linguistics*.[1] This was the school in which Noam Chomsky was trained and against which, in due course, he reacted.[2] Without going into details, we can simply list the following five principles or features as being characteristic of post-Bloomfieldian 'structuralism': (i) it was corpus-based (rejecting the distinction of *langue* and *parole*, which will be introduced and explained presently); (ii) it was taxonomic or classificatory, rather than explanatory; (iii) it excluded the study of meaning from linguistics proper; (iv) it was restricted to the description of what is now commonly referred to as surface structure in language; (v) it attempted to formulate a set of inductive discovery procedures for the analysis of languages. I shall not elaborate any of these points, since they are irrelevant to our main theme. Nor shall I go into the rights and wrongs of the criticisms that Chomsky and others have directed against post-Bloomfieldian 'structuralism'. What must be emphasized, however, is that, when Chomsky and his followers criticize 'structural linguistics' as theoretically and methodologically deficient, it is a temporally and locally restricted, though historically very important, form of structuralism that they usually have in mind.

In the second and more general sense of 'structuralism'—the sense in which the term is customarily understood in European linguistics and in the work of those American linguists who followed Boas and Sapir, rather than Bloomfield—there is no conflict, in principle at least, between structural linguistics and transformational-generative grammar. I have mentioned the post-Bloomfieldian sense of 'structuralism' in order to forestall the possibility of misunderstanding or confusion. From now on we shall be concerned solely with the more general and, as I am inclined to describe it, the more legitimate sense of the term: the sense that can be characterized succinctly as Saussurean. For, as we shall see, it is Ferdinand de Saussure[3] who is generally regarded as the founder of modern structural linguistics.

What, then, is the central thesis of Saussurean structuralism as far as language is concerned? To put it first at its most general, it is this: that every language is cut to a unique pattern and that the units out of which utterances are composed—more carefully, the units which we identify (or postulate as theoretical constructs) in the analysis of utterances—can be identified only in terms of their relationships with other units in the same language. We cannot first determine what these units are and then, at a subsequent stage of the investigation, inquire what structural relationships hold between them. Linguistic units derive both their existence and their essence from their interrelations. Every distinct language is a unique relational structure; and the units which we identify in describing a particular language—sounds, words, meanings, etc.—are but points in the structure, or network, of relations.

What I have just said is, I appreciate, very abstract, and at this level of abstraction or generality it is no doubt rather difficult to comprehend. Let me illustrate it first from phonology: the investigation of the structure, or patterning, of sound in English. How many sounds, we might ask, are there in the word *pit*? What are they, and how are they arranged or combined? It should be observed, first of all, that we are employing the term 'sound' in this context to refer to members of a set of linguistic units which we identify (or postulate as theoretical constructs) in the analysis of a particular language. Let us call these units *phonemes*; and let us assume that they are combined sequentially to form the words of the language. (There are other ways in which we can conceptualize and describe the phonological structure of languages. But we need not be concerned about these alternatives here.) As pronounced, the word *pit* consists of a continuous burst of sound, which the phonetician can analyse into a fairly large number of overlapping acoustic components. Physically speaking, the event which we refer to as the pronunciation of the word *pit* is not composed of a sequence of discrete units of sound. Furthermore, every pronunciation of the word, considered as a physical event, is somewhat different from every other pronunciation of the same word by different speakers and by the same speaker on different occasions. How do we identify it as the same word? What is the linguistic identity or constancy underlying the diversity of physical manifestation? The structuralist will reply that it is an identity of pattern or structure. Every acceptable pronunciation of *pit* is kept distinct from every acceptable pronunciation of such words as *bit*, *fit*, *hit*, *lit*, etc. by a variety of articulatory and acoustic differences at the beginning of the continuous bursts of sound in question; from every acceptable pronunciation of such words as *pet*, *pat*, etc. by differences in the middle of the bursts; and from every acceptable pronunciation of such words as *pick*, *pin*, etc. by differences at the end of the bursts. We might be tempted to say (and many linguistically unsophisticated people no doubt believe that this is the case) that there is a certain set of sounds (a *p*-sound, an *i*-sound, a *t*-sound, etc.) given in advance, as it were, from which all languages make their selection and which they modify in minor ways (so that a French *p*, for example, is essentially the same sound as an English *p*, but pronounced with more tension of the lips and without accompanying aspiration). The structuralist will deny that this is so. He will say that each language draws different distinctions in the continuum of sound and makes them functional, or linguistically relevant, by utilizing them to keep distinct such forms as *pit* and *bit*, *cap* and *cab*, etc. Consider a language in which what we can identify phonetically in the bursts of sound as [p] occurs only at the end of forms and what we can identify phonetically as [b] occurs only at the beginning. They might legitimately be regarded as alternative, positionally determined, realizations of the same phoneme: i.e. as instantiations of the same linguistic unit. What counts, then, in establishing the inventory of phonemes in any language is whether the bits of the phonetic complex correlated with them are in functional contrast or not. Phonemes are postulated, in the description of the language, as the terminals of these relations of functional contrast; they have no prior and independent existence.

As with phonology, so with grammar. Such grammatical categories as number (singular, plural, etc.), tense (past, present, future, etc.), or gender (masculine, feminine, neuter, etc.) may be fairly widespread in the languages of the world, but they are by no means universal; and the tense distinctions or gender distinctions drawn in one language may be quite different from those that are drawn in another. Each term in a grammatical category (e.g. past in the English category of tense) is in contrast with other terms in the same category in the same language (viz. non-past, or, under a different and more traditional analysis of tense in English, present and future). Past tense in French, for example, is no more identifiable with past tense in English than is a French '*p*-sound' with an English '*p*-sound'. The system of temporal distinctions that operates in French is different from the system that operates in English (and standard colloquial French differs from standard literary French in its categorization of past time). One can, of course, exaggerate the structural incommensurability of languages in their grammar, as also in their phonology and vocabulary; and many structuralists have undoubtedly been guilty of such exaggeration. I shall come back to this point. For the present, however, let me simply reiterate the structuralist thesis with respect to the grammatical structure of language without dilution or qualification: from the indefinitely many possible distinctions that could be made, each language selects a certain set, as it were, and *grammaticalizes* them in terms of such categories as tense, number, gender, case, person, proximity, visibility, shape, animacy, etc., and groups words, by different principles in different languages, into classes of the kind we refer to traditionally as parts of speech. But there is more to describing the grammatical structure of a language than merely identifying the categories operative in the language and grouping the words into parts of speech. We must also determine the rules or principles according to which the categories and word-classes are combined to form sentences, just as we must determine in phonology the rules or principles by which phonemes are combined to form words. By the grammatical structure of language is meant the network, or pattern, of functional relationships which hold between the grammatical categories and word classes—on the one hand, relationships of functional contrast and, on the other hand, combinatorial relationships. And once again it must be emphasized that the units of grammatical description (what we are, for simplicity, calling categories and word-classes) derive their linguistic validity from the place they occupy in this relational network and cannot be investigated or even identified independently of it.

Let us now pass on to consider briefly what is meant by structuralism with respect to the vocabularies of languages. The naïve monolingual speaker of English (or of any other language) might be forgiven for believing, as he may well do, that the meanings of words are, in principle, independent of the language he happens to speak and that the same meanings will be found correlated with the words of other languages. If this were the case, translation from one language to another would be a trivial exercise. Now anyone who has had any experience of translating knows that it is a far from trivial exercise and that word-for-word translation is generally unsatisfactory and frequently impossible. Not everyone, however, has drawn from this experience what the structuralist would regard as the correct and theoretically interesting conclusion. It is not simply that the one language *lexicalizes* (i.e. provides a word for) a small number of rather abstract concepts that are not lexicalized in the other (although this may indeed be true); nor is it because two or more meanings may be correlated with homonymous words in the one language, but not in the other, that word-for-word translation is difficult, and interestingly so. The theoretically significant point is this: the meaning of a word is a function of its relationship with other words in the same language, and the boundaries between the meanings of prima facie equivalent words in different languages may be, and very frequently are, incongruent.

Let us take just one example. Consider how we might translate into French the following English sentence (and I have deliberately selected what is perhaps the archetypical instance of linguistic banality): *The cat sat on the mat*. There is a problem straightaway with *sat*. Is the sentence being used to express the fact that the cat was in a certain position (*être assis*) or that it took up a certain position (*s'asseoir*)? Here, as elsewhere, French grammaticalizes a distinction that English does not. If we were translating the sentence into standard literary French rather than spoken colloquial French we should also be faced with the problem of selecting the right tense (*s'assit* or *s'est assis*, or even *s'asseyait*). But these differences between the two languages are matters of grammar rather than vocabulary. How do we translate *the cat*? As *le chat*, knowing that the animal being referred to was male or being ignorant of or unconcerned with its sex? Or as *la chatte* knowing that it was female? The fact that French will use *chatte* in reference to a female cat, known to be female, whereas English will not necessarily use a phrase like *tabby cat* in the same circumstances means that the distinction between *cat, tom cat*, and *tabby cat* in English does not match the distinction drawn between *chat* and *chatte* in French at any point. This may seem to be a trivial enough example of the difference between the meanings of roughly equivalent words in the two languages; and indeed it is. But it is typical of many such differences; and they all illustrate the same point. Consider, now, the translation of *mat*. Is it a door-mat that we are referring to (*paillasson*), or a bedside mat (*descente de lit*), or a small rug (*tapis*)—not to mention various other possibilities? There is a set of words in English, *mat, rug, carpet*, etc., and a set of words in French, *tapis, paillasson, carpette*, etc.; and none of the French words has the same meaning as any one of the English words. Each set of words divides a certain part of the universe of domestic furnishings, as it were, in a different way; the two systems of categorization are incommensurate. It does not follow of course that in practice we cannot translate satisfactorily enough between the two languages. For what we do when we translate is to determine, as best we can, how the objects, events, and processes being referred to would be categorized in terms of a more or less similar, but frequently incongruent, system of distinctions and equivalences. But the meanings of the words we choose are internal to the language in which we conduct the categorization and express ourselves.

The structuralist conception of vocabulary that I have just presented has been challenged recently, in a particularly interesting way, by Brent Berlin and Paul Kay in their book *Basic Color Terms*.[4] I shall come back to their criticisms later. But first I must introduce and explain four Saussurean dichotomies that have been of great importance in the development of structural linguistics.

The first is the dichotomy of *substance* and *form* (to use Saussure's own terms). This is very similar to the Aristotelian and scholastic distinction of matter and form. (It is perhaps terminologically unfortunate that Saussure employed the expression 'substance', rather than 'matter', since 'substance' is opposed to both 'matter' and 'form', and has a quite different sense, in the philosophical tradition which derives from Aristotle. But in modern scientific and colloquial usage 'matter' has, of course, acquired the restricted sense of something with a spatio-temporal extension; and we must abstract from this more particular connotation of the term in our interpretation of the Saussurean concept of 'substance'.) Substance is the substratum of variation and individuality. It has no existence, or actuality, independently of form; but it can be logically distinguished from form in the scientific analysis of the nature, or essence, of things. To take a familiar and traditional example: when a sculptor carves a statue out of a block of marble, he takes something which, from the present point of view, we may think of as being shapeless and internally undifferentiated and gives to it, by the process of sculpting, a definite and distinctive shape, so that it becomes, for example, a statue of Apollo or Pegasus. The marble, considered as substance, is potentially many things, but actually it is none; it becomes one thing rather than another by the imposition of one form rather than another on the undifferentiated substratum. So it is, says Saussure, with language. But languages result from the imposition of form on two different kinds of substance: sound and thought. The phonological composition of a word—what Saussure called the *signifiant* (that which has meaning)—is a complex of phonemes, each of which, as we have seen, derives its essence and existence from the structure (i.e. form) imposed by that language upon the continuum (i.e. substance) of sound. The meaning of a word—more precisely that aspect of the meaning of a word which Saussure identified as the *signifié* (its sense, rather than its denotation or reference) derives from the imposition of structure on the *a priori* nebulous and inchoate continuum of thought. Word-forms and meanings have no existence, as units, outside the particular languages in which they are actualized. Nor does either exist independently of the other. For every word-form is coupled with at least one meaning; and each meaning is associated with at least one word-form. (The qualification 'at least one' allows for the possibility of homonymy and polysemy, on the one hand, and of synonymy, on the other.) The combination of a certain word-form with a certain meaning yields a linguistic *sign.*

Saussure's distinction of substance and form is crucial in what one may think of as mainstream structuralism. Not all structuralists, however, have employed the same terms as he did. The term 'structure' itself has generally been used in place of 'form'; and it is indeed a more appropriate term in view of the many other senses that 'form' has in linguistics and other disciplines. And many scholars have described meaning in language in terms of the categorization of 'reality' or of 'the world' rather than in terms of the imposition of form upon the substance of thought or conceptual content. Structuralism can be associated with either phenomenalism or idealism, or indeed explicitly dissociated (as it was, for example, by Hjelmslev, *Prolegomena to a Theory of Language*)[5] from both. We need not be concerned here with these varying interpretations of the substratum of meaning, important though they undoubtedly are.

The second of Saussure's dichotomies has to do with the relationships which hold between signs (and, at the level of phonology, between the components of word-forms). These are of two kinds: *syntagmatic* and *paradigmatic.* ('Paradigmatic' is in fact Hjelmslev's term, but it is now more commonly employed than Saussure's term 'associative'.) The syntagmatic relations which an element contracts are those which derive from its combination with preceding and following elements of the same level. For example, the word *old* is syntagmatically related with the preceding word *the* and with the following word *man* in the syntagm, or construction, *the old man*; the phoneme /i/ is syntagmatically related with the preceding /p/ and the following /t/ in the word *pit*, phonologically represented as /pit/. The paradigmatic relations contracted by an element are those which hold between the actually occurring element and other elements of the same level which might have occurred in its place. For example, *young, tall*, etc. might equally well have occurred in the context *the . . . man* and by virtue of this fact are in paradigmatic relationship with *old* in the context *the . . . man.* Similarly, the phonemes /e/ or /a/ might have occurred, and are thus in paradigmatic relationship with /i/, in the context /p-t/. All this is obvious enough; and it is only too easy, as generations of scholars have done through the ages, to pass over these simple facts without appreciating their significance. The theoretically important point is that the structure of language at every level depends upon the complementary principles of selection and combination. The set of paradigmatically related, or interchangeable, elements that can occur in one context is typically distinct from the set of elements that can occur in another context. We identify elements—phonemes, words, or whatever—by virtue of their potentiality for occurrence in certain combinations; and the selection of one element rather than another produces a different resultant syntagm with a characteristically different meaning (due allowance being made for the free variation of phonemes, in certain contexts, and for synonymy). To describe a language is to specify both the membership of the paradigmatic sets and the possibilities of combination of one set with another in well-formed constructions. Looked at from this point of view, languages can be seen, at each level of analysis, as having two dimensions, or axes, of structure; and every element has its place at one or more points in this two-dimensional structure. Modern linguistics has gone far beyond Saussure in its explication of the notion of syntagmatic relationship. Generative grammar, in particular, has provided a much richer and more powerful notion of combination than that of mere successivity. But it is still based upon the Saussurean principle of the interdependence of the paradigmatic and the syntagmatic in language.

We now come to the third of Saussure's distinctions: between language considered as *langue* and language considered as *parole*. There are no generally accepted English equivalents for these terms, but Chomsky has recently drawn a very similar distinction between linguistic competence and linguistic performance. I shall use the terms language-system and language-behaviour. What is it, we might ask, that the linguist sets out to describe in his description of a particular natural language? Is it the actual utterances produced by native speakers on particular occasions? No, says Saussure, it is the system of regularities which underlies the utterances produced by speakers that the linguist should make the object of his description: the language-system (*langue*), not actual language-behaviour (*parole*). It is the language-system that is structured in terms of paradigmatic and syntagmatic relations, and it is only derivatively with reference to this underlying system that we recognize actual utterances as being composed of certain elements arranged in a certain way. There is much in Saussure's doctrine of the language-system that is unclear; and the precise nature of the distinction he wished to establish has been the subject of considerable controversy. Saussure emphasized the supraindividual and social character of the language-system; and yet he also insisted that it was not a purely abstract construct of the linguist —that it was stored, in some sense, in the brain of every member of the speech-community. We need not go into these details here. It is sufficient to have drawn the distinction in fairly general terms. Linguists will argue about the degree of abstraction and idealization involved in the postulation of an underlying, relatively uniform, language-system; and many of them will deny that the system they postulate is internalized, as such, in the nervous system of the native speakers of the language they are describing. But few linguists, nowadays, operate without drawing some kind of distinction between language-behaviour and the system of units and relations underlying that behaviour; and it is the structure of the underlying system that they would claim to be describing.

Little need be said, in this context, about the fourth Saussurean dichotomy: between the *synchronic* and the *diachronic* investigation of languages. By the synchronic analysis of language is meant the investigation of the structure of that language (i.e. the language-system) as it is, or was, at a given point in time; by the diachronic analysis of a language is to be understood the study of changes in the language between two given periods in time. The methodological importance of this principle for linguistics lies in the fact that, until quite recently, it was quite common for scholars to take texts from widely separated periods (from Shakespeare and from Dickens, shall we say) and to treat them as being written in the same language. If we apply strictly the distinction of the synchronic and the diachronic, we shall say that two different language-systems underlie the texts of different periods; that each of these systems can be studied, synchronically, independently of the other; and that diachronic linguistics can then investigate how the earlier system was transformed into the later. There are of course complications; especially when the texts of an earlier period are familiar to, and understood and quoted by, speakers at a later period. But this does not affect the validity of the principle that every language operates, at a given point in time, as an independent system; and that the history of language is synchronically irrelevant. One should, however, stress the fact that the distinction of the synchronic and the diachronic can only be sensibly applied with respect to periods relatively well separated in time. Two dialects spoken at the same time may differ from one another more significantly than two diachronically distinct states of what we should regard as the same language or dialect. In fact, the truth of the matter is that language-change can be seen as but one aspect of language-variation; and the dimensions of language-variation are geographical and social, as well as temporal. When we talk of a speech-community existing in a particular place at a particular point in time we are not using the expression 'point in time' in a literal sense. The speech-community, in this sense, is an abstraction, or idealization. It is just as much a theoretical construct of the linguist as is the uniform language-system which it presupposes and is presupposed by; and it rests upon the more or less deliberate, and to some degree arbitrary, discounting of variations in the language-behaviour of those who are held, pretheoretically, to speak 'the same language'.

The ideas of Saussure were taken up by many different schools of linguists in the years that followed upon the publication of his posthumous *Cours de linguistique générale*. It is not possible here to discuss, or even to mention, their various points of agreement and disagreement. But there is one further notion that should be introduced which, though it is not to be found in Saussure, has been associated with at least two of the major European schools of post-Saussurean structural linguistics, the Prague School (represented by such scholars as N. S. Trubetskoy and Roman Jakobson) and the Copenhagen School (headed by Louis Hjelmslev), and is currently incorporated in Chomsky's theory of generative grammar and S. Lamb's theory of stratificational grammar in the United States. I am referring to the view that the phonemes and the meanings of words in different languages can be analysed into components, or *distinctive features*, of sound and meaning and that, although the complexes of components (i.e. the phonemes and word-meanings) and the paradigmatic and syntagmatic interrelations of these complexes are unique to particular languages, the components themselves are universal. In other words, neither the substance of sound nor the substance of meaning is an undifferentiated continuum within which languages draw arbitrary distinctions. What we have in each case, it is maintained, is a set of potential distinctions, a subset of which is actualized by each language. This thesis, as I have just presented it, is empirically indistinguishable from the Saussurean thesis of the continuity of substance. It becomes more interesting, as an alternative, when it is coupled with the further proposition that there is some 'natural' hierarchy in the sets of components such that all languages will actualize certain distinctions of sound and meaning more readily than others. For this proposition is undoubtedly in conflict with what has been, historically, one of the most characteristic and most challenging aspects of structuralism in linguistics: its insistence that the actualization of particular phonological and semantic distinctions in different language-systems is completely arbitrary. This is what is usually meant by the assertion that there are no substantive universals of language; and it is probably fair to say that this is a proposition to which, until recently, most European and American linguists would have subscribed. It can be referred to as the doctrine of linguistic relativity.

It is the doctrine of linguistic relativity in the domain of semantics that Berlin and Kay set out to challenge in their book on colour terminology referred to earlier. I shall give a brief exposition of their work and then, assuming for the purpose of the argument that their findings and the conclusions that they draw from them are correct, attempt to assess their relevance for structuralism. It is a well-established fact, which Berlin and Kay do not dispute, that word-for-word translation of colour terms across languages is frequently impossible: for example, there is no single word for the English *blue* in Russian; there is no single word for *brown* in French; some languages have only two basic colour terms, others have only three or four, whereas English (according to Berlin and Kay) has eleven. The situation with respect to the vocabulary of colour is, in this respect, typical of what was said to hold for the vocabulary as a whole, earlier in this chapter. What Berlin and Kay maintain is that there are eleven psycho-physically definable areas in the continuum of colour, which we may label with the English words (1) *black*, (2) *white*, (3) *red*, (4) *green*, (5) *yellow*, (6) *blue*, (7) *brown*, (8) *purple*, (9) *pink*, (10) *orange*, (11) *grey*, and that these are the focal areas for the vocabulary of colour in all languages. Although different languages contain different numbers of basic colour terms, there is a 'natural' hierarchy in the eleven universal focal areas which determines their lexicalization in any language; and this hierarchy is represented in the order in which I have listed the focal areas above (as far as the sixth or seventh—there is no ordering posited for the colours listed from (8) to (11) above). The 'naturalness' of the ordering of colours is reflected in the fact that all languages with only two basic colour terms have words whose focal point is in the area of black and white (rather than, say, in yellow and purple); all languages with only three basic colour terms have words for black, white, and red (but no basic word for green or blue); all four-term languages (if I may so use the expression in this context) have words for black, white, red, and either green or yellow; all five-term languages have words for black, white, red, green, and yellow (green and yellow are only partially ordered in relation to one another and to the other colours); and so on. It may also be a fact, but so far the evidence is not available, that children learn the denotation of colour terms in the same 'natural' order (to the point that their native language lexicalizes the basic psychophysical categories), first mastering the distinction of black and white, then learning red, afterwards green or yellow, and so on.

Now, Berlin and Kay's work can be, and has been, criticized on various grounds; and it would be premature, to say the least, to accept their hypothesis as well confirmed. But confirmation of the hypothesis, or of some hypothesis different in detail but similar in its general import, may yet be forthcoming. Let us take it as it stands and see what conclusions we can draw from it.

The main point to be made, and it is of the greatest importance for the structuralist, is that Berlin and Kay have made clear the necessity of distinguishing between the total extension of a term and its focal extension. Two languages might well differ with respect to the boundaries that they draw between the meanings of words and yet be in agreement with respect to what is focal in the meaning of 'roughly equivalent' words. This might be the case (I do not know) with words like *chair* and *chaise*, or *carpet* and *tapis*, in English and French. If so, their focal equivalence would be reflected in the fact (if it is a fact) that, asked to point to or describe a typical 'chair' and a typical 'chaise', respectively, the English-speaker and the French-speaker would point to or describe the same kind of object. It seems to me undeniable that, in the past, structuralists have been inclined to overemphasize the importance of determining where the boundaries are drawn between contiguous areas of a continuum. But the phenomenal world as we perceive it is not an undifferentiated continuum; and the way in which it is categorized conceptually and linguistically might very well depend upon our recognition of certain focal types of colour, shape, texture, biological and social functions, and so on. It is noteworthy, in this connection, that when asked to define colour words (other than in the sophisticated terms of psychology and physics) we frequently operate by means of comparison with familiar entities of our everyday experience; red is the colour of blood, green the colour of grass, and so on. Nor should it be forgotten that even the continuum of colour is itself a very sophisticated concept. The world created by modern technology, with its profusion of colours of different shades in dress, furnishings, paintings, book-jackets, and other artefacts, is very untypical of the world in which man has lived throughout most of his history. The natural world of flora and fauna, of sea, sky, woods, and pasture, leaves much of the colour space unfilled. If there are indeed a limited number of universal psychophysical focal colour points it seems plausible to assume that these correlate with the characteristic colours of salient objects in man's physical and cultural habitat.

I have just introduced the notion of 'salience'; and I shall use this to modify the more traditional version of structuralism which I have expounded in the earlier part of this paper. All men, wherever they are born and in whatever culture they are reared, are genetically endowed, we may assume, with the same perceptual and conceptual predispositions, at least to the extent that these genetic predispositions determine the acquisition of linguistically pertinent distinctions of sound and meaning. This assumption has at times been challenged, but it has not been disproved; and the evidence at present available would suggest that any child, whatever his parentage might be, is capable of learning any language, provided that he is brought up in an environment in which this language is employed for all the multifarious activities of everyday life. By virtue of his perceptual and conceptual predispositions the child will notice certain aspects of his environment rather than others. Such aspects of the environment may be described as biologically salient; and it is within the province of cognitive psychology and neuro-physiology to determine why and how they are perceptually and conceptually salient. It is possible, as has been hypothesized, that there is fixed maturational sequence in the acquisition of certain perceptual and conceptual distinctions; and, if this is so, it could be at least one factor responsible for the 'natural' hierarchy in distinctions of sound and meaning found in the languages of the world. For example, the greater saliency of variations in luminosity (coupled with the biological importance of the succession of day and night in human life) could account for the universal recognition of the distinction of black and white; the neurophysiological basis for the distinction of reddish and greenish hues might account for the place of words for these focal areas in the vocabulary of colour; and so on.

Superimposed upon the biologically given hierarchy of perceptual and conceptual saliency, however, there is another kind of saliency, which depends upon and extends it, and which may at particular points be in partial conflict with it. This is what may be called cultural saliency. Every language is integrated with the culture in which it operates; and the word-meanings which a language establishes are structured in terms of distinctions that are important in that culture. (This may also be true of some of the grammatical categories in languages; but it is not the case, it would appear, for phonological units.) By being brought up in a certain culture, and, as part of this process of acculturation, learning the language operating in that culture, the child comes to acquire the culturally salient features; and, once again, he may do so in a hierarchically determined manner. For some anthropologists, at least, have maintained that there are universals of culture, just as there are biologically determined universals of cognition.

When due allowance has been made, however, for the influence of biological and cultural saliency in determining the substantive universals of language-systems, there still appears to be a considerable part of the structure of all languages which, on present evidence at least, does not appear to be so determined. The structuralist thesis (in a duly modified form), that every language-system is unique though it may have a universal substructure, has not lost its validity. Nor indeed is it affected by the particular form of universalism advocated by Chomsky and his followers, according to which the universals of language structure, both formal and substantive, are determined, not by general biological and cultural factors of the kind referred to above, but by a species-specific human capacity for the acquisition of language as such. Generative grammar, whether it is conceived more widely as a theory of the nature of language or more narrowly as a formalization of the paradigmatic and syntagmatic relations holding between linguistic units, has enriched, but it has not supplanted or outmoded, Saussurean structuralism.

NOTES

1. University of Chicago Press, Chicago, 1951.
2. Cf. J. Lyons, *Chomsky* (Fontana, London, 1970).
3. *Cours de linguistique générale* (Payot, Paris, 1916).
4. B. Berlin and P. Kay, *Basic Color Terms* (University of California Press, Berkeley, 1969).
5. L. Hjelmslev, *Prolegomena to a Theory of Language*, tr. F. J. Whitfield, *International Journal of American Linguistics, Memoir VII* (Baltimore, Md., 1953).

# 2 *The Linguistic Basis of Structuralism*

JONATHAN CULLER

STRUCTURE, we are repeatedly told, is not an abstract form but content itself, grasped in its logical organization; but seldom is this article of faith more blatantly flouted than in general discussions of structuralism, where the relations of part and whole, suggested by the titles of various contributions (Structuralism and Linguistics, Structuralism and Anthropology, Structuralism and Literature) often fail to materialize in the articles themselves. When the ferrets from each discipline are loosed for this hunt they do not converge upon a common rabbit but pursue their own hares in divergent, criss-crossing tunnels. And the observers often feel that despite the elegance of the proceedings no common quarry has been flushed. They depart with nothing—no common method or theory—that they can point to and call 'structuralism'.

It may be, of course, that the term has outlived its usefulness. To call oneself a structuralist was always a polemical gesture, a way of attracting attention and associating oneself with others whose work was of moment; and, therefore, by the time structuralism became the subject of colloquia it had taken so many guises that little could be gained from using the term. This is the conclusion one is tempted to draw, for example, from Jean Piaget's *Structuralism*, which shows that mathematics, logic, physics, biology, and all the social sciences have long been concerned with structure and were practising 'structuralism' before the coming of Lévi-Strauss. But this use of the term leaves unexplained one important fact: why, in this case, did French structuralism seem new and exciting? Even if it be set down as just another Paris fashion, that alone would argue some striking and differentiating qualities. There are, at least, prima facie reasons for assuming that there was something distinctive about the work of a few central figures, such as Barthes and Lévi-Strauss. So before accepting Piaget's conclusions and following 'structure' and 'structuralism' on their picaresque adventures through the various disciplines, one might try to isolate a central doctrinal core and give structuralism a specific meaning which the reader might use to draw together the essays in this volume. And if this seems rather like pulling the rabbit out of a hat, one might at least hope that when dissected it will bear some resemblance to the hares coursed in other essays.

Roland Barthes once defined structuralism as a method for the study of cultural artefacts which originates in the methods of contemporary linguistics.[1] This view can be supported both from structuralist texts, such as Lévi-Strauss's pioneering article, 'L'Analyse structurale en linguistique et en anthropologie', which argued that by following the linguist's example the anthropologist might reproduce in his own discipline the 'phonological revolution', and from the work of structuralism's most serious and able opponents. To attack structuralism, Paul Ricœur argues, one must focus discussion on its linguistic foundations.[2] Moreover, this definition has the virtue of posing several obvious questions: Why should linguistics be relevant to the study of other cultural phenomena? In what way is it relevant? What are the effects of this linguistic orientation? What are the results of using linguistic concepts and procedures in other fields? An answer to the first two questions would be a statement of structuralist theory and an answer to the last two an account of structuralist method.

The notion that linguistics might be useful in studying other cultural phenomena is based on two fundamental insights: first, that social and cultural phenomena are signs, and secondly, that they do not have essences but are defined by a network of relations, both internal and external. Stress may fall on one or the other of these propositions—it would be in these terms, for example, that one might try to distinguish between semiology and structuralism—but in fact the two are inseparable, for in studying signs one must investigate the system of relations which enables meaning to be produced, and, reciprocally, the pertinent relations between items can be determined only if one considers them as signs.

Thus structuralism is based, in the first instance, on the realization that if human actions or productions have a meaning there must be an underlying system of conventions which makes this meaning possible. Confronted with a marriage ceremony or a game of football, for example, an observer with no knowledge of the culture in question could present an objective description of the actions which took place, but he would be unable to grasp their meaning and so would not be treating them as social or cultural phenomena. The actions are meaningful only with respect to a set of institutional conventions. Wherever there are two posts one can kick a ball between them, but one can score a goal only within a particular institutionalized framework. As Lévi-Strauss writes, 'les conduites individuelles ne sont jamais symboliques par elles-mêmes: elles sont des éléments à partir desquels un système symbolique, qui ne peut être que collectif, se construit.'[3] The cultural meaning of any particular act or object is determined by a whole system of constitutive rules—rules which do not so much regulate behaviour as create the possibility of particular forms of behaviour. The rules of English enable sequences of sound to have meaning; they make it possible to utter grammatical or ungrammatical sentences. And, analogously, various social rules make it possible to marry, to score a goal, to write a poem, to be impolite. It is in this sense that a culture is composed of a set of symbolic systems.

But why should linguistics, the study of one particular and rather distinctive system, be thought to provide methods for investigating any symbolic system? Saussure considered this problem when he came to postulate the need for a science of 'semiology'—a general science of signs. He argued that although the meanings of many actions or objects may seem natural, they are always founded on shared assumptions or conventions. Though this is obvious in the case of linguistic signs, it is also true of other signs, and therefore by taking linguistics as a model one may avoid the familiar mistake of assuming that signs which appear natural to those who use them have an intrinsic meaning and require no explanation. Linguistics, designed to study the systems of rules underlying speech, will by its very nature compel the analyst to attend to the conventional basis of the phenomena he is investigating.[4]

When he does so he will find himself, like the linguist, dealing with relations and therefore with structures. If a particular action is impolite it is not because of its intrinsic qualities but because of certain relational features which differentiate it from polite actions. For Lévi-Strauss this refusal to treat terms as independent entities, the insistence on the primacy of relations between terms, was one of the major lessons which anthropologists should learn from linguistics and particularly from phonology. Indeed Trubetzkoy, in the work which laid the foundations of phonology, showed his awareness of the important methodological implications of his theory for the social sciences. Whereas the phonetician is concerned with the properties of actual speech-sounds, the phonologist is interested in the differential features which are functional in a particular language, the relations between sounds which enable speakers of a language to distinguish between words.

> La phonologie doit rechercher quelles différences phoniques sont liées, dans la langue étudiée, à des différences de signification, comment les éléments de différenciation (ou marques) se comportent entre eux et selon quelles règles ils peuvent se combiner les uns avec les autres pour former des mots ou des phrases.[5]

It is clear, he continues, that these tasks cannot be accomplished by the methods of the natural sciences, which are concerned with the intrinsic properties of phenomena themselves and not with the differential features which are bearers of social significance. In other words, in the natural sciences there is nothing corresponding to the distinction between *langue* and *parole*: there is no institution or system to be studied. The social sciences, on the other hand, are concerned with the social use of material objects and must therefore distinguish between the objects themselves and the system of distinctive or differential features which give them meaning and value. Attempts to describe such systems, Trubetzkoy argues, are closely analogous to work in phonology. The example he cites is the ethnological study of clothing. Many features of particular physical garments which would be of considerable importance to the wearer are of no interest to the ethnologist, who is concerned only with those features that carry a social significance. Length of skirts might be an important differential feature in the fashion-system of a culture, while the materials from which they were made were not. The ethnologist tries to reconstruct the system of relations and distinctions which members of that society have assimilated and which they display in taking certain garments as indicating a particular life-style or social condition. He is interested in those relations by which garments are made into signs.

In insisting that the methods of linguistics and the social sciences were different from those of the natural sciences, Trubetzkoy was denying the suggestions of some linguists that phonemes were comparable to taxonomic classes in botany or zoology. One can classify animals in various ways: according to size, habitat, bone structure, phylogeny. But, though some taxonomies may be more useful than others, there is no *correct* taxonomy. In the case of linguistics and other social sciences, however, one cannot simply group items together on the basis of observed similarities. One must determine what are the real functional classes of the system in question. However great the similarities between two sounds, one can class them together as realizations of a single phoneme only if they do not serve to differentiate two words in the language. If one has classed aspirated and unaspirated /p/ as variants of a single phoneme one must justify this choice by showing that the difference between them is never in the language used to distinguish one word from another.

Trubetzkoy's point is an important one which has only recently been given its due. Linguistics is not a taxonomic science, because its descriptive classes, unlike those of a taxonomy, can be right or wrong. They are right or wrong as descriptions of the system which speakers of a language have assimilated. In short, linguistics does not simply divide sentences into units; it aspires in its identification of units to describe speakers' implicit knowledge of a language. As Chomsky says, enunciating the fundamental principle of linguistic description, 'without reference to this tacit knowledge there is no such subject as descriptive linguistics. There is nothing for its descriptive statements to be right or wrong about.'[6] A language is not simply a collection of sentences, for there are well-formed sentences of English that have never been uttered, and an adequate description of English would have to account for these potential grammatical and ungrammatical sentences. The language must therefore be considered as a system of items and rules that have been assimilated by native speakers; a description of the language is an explicit representation of their implicit knowledge. The facts which linguistics must explain are various, but they are all facts about this implicit knowledge: that any sentence on this page, read backwards, is not a well-formed English sentence, that *Flying planes can be dangerous* is ambiguous, that *The enemy destroyed the city* and *The city was destroyed by the enemy* are synonymous, and so on. One might say, by analogy, that the sociologist or anthropologist attempts to explicate the implicit knowledge which enables people to function as members of a particular group or society. The facts to be explained are, again, facts about this knowledge: that a particular action is taboo whereas another is permitted, that given objects have a certain significance whereas others have different meanings. Where there is knowledge or mastery of any kind, there is a system to be explained. This is the fundamental principle that guides one's extrapolation from linguistics into other disciplines. If the meanings assigned to objects or actions are not purely random phenomena, then there must be a system of distinctions, categories, and operations to be described.

The other linguistic terms and concepts, which help to identify structuralist prose, are inessential compared to this basic methodological orientation. The linguistic model suggests that the task of structuralists, whatever their field, is not to describe a corpus of data or to construct taxonomies but to examine the set of underlying relations through which things can function as signs. The goal is to make explicit the implicit knowledge used in the recognition and reading of signs.

One might sketch the implications of this approach by looking briefly at structuralist work in four fairly diverse areas: anthropology, the history and philosophy of science, the study of popular culture, and literary criticism. The following rudimentary discussions do not aim to document the achievement of structuralism in these fields but only to indicate the similarities among these enterprises which can be attributed to a common foundation in the analogy with linguistics.

In the field of anthropology, first of all, one might cite Mary Douglas's *Purity and Danger* as a brilliant and impeccable example of a structuralism intent on its object and unencumbered by a rebarbative terminology. In studying laws and practices relating to pollution and taboo Professor Douglas tries in each case to reconstruct a total system of classification which would account for the prohibitions and exclusions practised by a particular society. 'Where there is dirt there is system. Dirt is the by-product of a systematic ordering and classification of matter.'[7] Members of the society need not be aware of the functional distinctions and classes, 'any more than speakers are able to be explicit about the linguistic patterns they employ',[8] but in both cases their practical mastery of the system, their knowledge of what is acceptable and unacceptable, provides the evidence needed to devise an account of the system.

Her discussion of the abominations of Leviticus provides an admirable case in point. 'Why should the camel, the hare and the rock badger be unclean? Why should some locusts, but not all, be unclean? Why should the frog be clean and the mouse and hippopotamus unclean? What have chameleons, moles and crocodiles got in common that they should be listed together? (Leviticus 11:27.)'[9] *Ad hoc*, piecemeal explanations are unsatisfactory. One wants a systematic explanation which accounts for all the prohibitions by setting out a group of rules which are consciously or unconsciously employed. There seem, in fact, to be two basic rules. First of all, 'cloven-hoofed, cud-chewing ungulates are the model of the proper kind of food for a pastoralist.'[10] Animals which meet one of these conditions but not the other are improper anomalies and hence unholy. The pig is forbidden because it has cloven hooves but does not chew its cud; its supposedly filthy habits have nothing to do with the case. The hare and the rock badger, which were thought to be ruminant, are excluded because they lack cloven hooves. When neither of these features is present another rule applies: Biblical cosmology defines three classes of animals, and any creature that does not wholly conform to its class is impure. 'In the firmament two-legged fowls fly with wings. In the water scaly fish swim with fins. On the earth four-legged animals hop, jump, or walk. Any class of creatures which is not equipped for the right kind of locomotion in its element is contrary to holiness.'[11] Fish without fins are prohibited. Creatures that 'swarm' are anomalous, but any locust that hops is clean, as is the frog. The crocodile, the mouse, the mole, and the chameleon are unclean because they appear to have two feet and two hands yet go upon all fours. And one can predict that if penguins had been known in the Middle East they would have been taboo as wingless (and therefore impure) birds. Were there any 'native speakers' available, one could test the explanatory hypothesis by determining whether its predictions accorded with their judgements.

Such an approach emphasizes the importance of gathering evidence about the meaning of particular items for a given group, for the goal is the reconstruction of the system of conventions which is operative for members of that group. This is a point occasionally lost sight of in theoretical discussions. For example, Lévi-Strauss argues that anthropology is a branch of semiology in that the phenomena it studies are signs, but the example he cites is highly suspect: a stone axe is a sign because it *stands for* something; to the observer with knowledge of other cultures it stands for the different tools which they would use for the same purpose.[12] But to consider the axe in this way is to make it an index, not a sign. If a tribe use stone axes to cut down trees they have no metal technology, and the axe is therefore an index of a particular cultural level. But this meaning is causal rather than conventional. To study the axe as a sign the analyst must consider its significance for members of the tribe; and these meanings, produced by the conventions of social life, will in turn provide evidence which helps him to construct a model of the underlying cultural system. The system of signs must be the system of a particular group, otherwise there is nothing to explain.

Michel Foucault's work in the history and philosophy of science obeys a similar imperative: his task is to draw from their obscurity 'les codes fondamentaux d'une culture' which define the objects of knowledge and hence determine the possible sciences of a period. Just as the conventional nature of the linguistic sign guarantees the presence of a system of some sort, so Foucault's enterprise is made possible by a sense of the arbitrariness and conventionality of any kind of order. The *episteme* of the Renaissance is different from that of the Classical period, which is in turn displaced by the set of assumptions and formation rules that governs our own scientific discourse. The fact that it has changed makes it open to analysis as a set of tacit conventions. In the Renaissance, for example, the basic conception of order is founded on the notion of resemblance: relations of similitude and analogy link together the microcosm and macrocosm, heaven and earth, the book of the world and the books of men. 'Chercher le sens c'est mettre au jour ce qui se ressemble.'[13] In the Classical period, however, the notion of representation displaces that of resemblance; the world is ordered not by qualitative, symbolic correspondences but by quantifiable identities and differences. It is the era of taxonomies, in which science is concerned with the representation of the order determined by visible characteristics.

The *episteme* of a period blocks certain types of investigation which might count as science in other times. For example, the philological, mythological, and literary research of a Renaissance naturalist like Aldrovandi was incomprehensible to Buffon, the great naturalist of the Classical period: to grant equal status in an account of the serpent to mythological, etymological, anatomical, heraldic, and anecdotal information could not but seem a scientific scandal. For Aldrovandi nature was an unbroken tissue of words and signs, and his task was to compile all the signs deposited on and around the animal, whether in the book of the world or in the books of men. For Buffon, on the other hand, language was not part of the world but a way of representing it: what had been said about an animal was of a radically different order from the animal's own characteristics. Buffon's incomprehension provides evidence about the formation rules which governed the possible scientific discourse of that period.

Indeed, just as in anthropology or linguistics it is the forbidden or the ungrammatical which offers the most promising material for studying the operative conventions and their limits, so for Foucault it is the inconceivable or the outrageous that is crucial. *Les Mots et les choses* opens with a text of Borges giving the classification of animals in an imaginary Chinese encyclopaedia: belonging to the Emperor, embalmed, sucking-pigs, fabulous, stray dogs, drawn with a camel-hair brush, etc. The impossibility of thinking this, except as an ironic *exemplum*, addresses a question to our own modes of classification:

> Quand nous disons que le chat et le chien se ressemblent moins que deux levriers, même s'ils sont l'un et l'autre apprivoisés ou embaumés, . . . quel est donc le sol à partir de quoi nous pouvons l'établir en toute certitude? Sur quelle 'table', selon quel espace d'identités, de similitudes, d'analogies, avons-nous pris l'habitude de distribuer tant de choses différentes et pareilles? Quelle est cette cohérence—dont on voit bien tout de suite qu'elle n'est ni déterminée par un enchaînement a priori et nécessaire, ni imposée par des contenus immédiatement sensibles?[14]

To discover the system of rules which govern our conceptual space and that of other periods is not, of course, an easy task: such norms are deeply sedimented, constituting as they do the limits of our intellectual world. But the difficulty is nothing new: the rules of a generative grammar are not revealed by introspection and are more complex than anything the native speaker might consciously imagine. Nor is the evidence fundamentally different: one's sense of the well-formed and the deviant designates limits that must be formulated.

In the study of mass culture the evidence is nearer to hand and the results less interesting, but the basic method is similar. It is a matter of determining the categories, the stereotypes and distinctions, through which a culture gives meaning to the world. What are the conventions used to produce the kind of meaning objects and events have in popular culture? Once again, this involves treating phenomena as signs and testing hypotheses by their ability to account for meanings which seem to us natural and appropriate. But precisely because in this case there is lacking the initial experience of strangeness which, when we are dealing with spatially or temporally distant cultures, convinces us of the existence of operative conventions, a strong theory is especially necessary if in studying contemporary myths or collective representations we are to overcome the temptation of taking the meanings of our culture for granted. The student of popular culture invariably finds himself charged with excessive ingenuity for offering elaborate explanations where none seem required. Should he attempt to explain why our guide-books have developed an insistent mythology of the picturesque, which cherishes mountains, gorges, swift-running streams, but neglects plains, valleys, and plateaux, he will be told, with a fine indignation, that mountains simply *are* picturesque and that no more need be said. His task is inevitably, then, one of demystification: to make us see that the meanings we take as natural are the historical products of a cultural system. He is guided in his work by a general theory of semiotic systems which insists that meaning is diacritical: if it means anything to call mountains picturesque then there must be other possibilities which are excluded by the conventions of the particular system he is studying.

Barthes's brilliant discussion of wrestling in *Mythologies* is a good example.[15] The sceptic might argue that wrestling is objectively different from boxing and therefore quite naturally has different meanings associated with it, but one can easily imagine a culture in which the two sports shared a single myth and were watched in the same way. In our own culture, however, there is clearly a difference in ethos which requires explanation. Why does one bet on boxing but not on wrestling? Why would it be odd for a boxer to scream and writhe in agony when hit, as wrestlers do? Why are rules consistently broken in wrestling but not in boxing? These differences are to be explained by a complex set of cultural conventions which make wrestling a spectacle rather than a contest. Boxing, Barthes says, is a Jansenist sport based on the demonstration of excellence: interest is directed towards the final outcome and visible suffering would be read only as a sign of imminent defeat. Wrestling, on the other hand, is drama in which each moment must be immediately intelligible as spectacle; the wrestlers themselves are physical caricatures cast in moral roles, and the outcome is of interest only for that reason. And thus while in boxing rules are external to the match, designating limits beyond which it must not go, in wrestling they are very much within it, as conventions which increase the range of meanings that can be produced. Rules exist to be violated, so that the 'bastard' may be more violently characterized and the audience engaged in revengeful fury. They are broken visibly (though the referee's back may be turned): a violation hidden from the audience would be pointless. Suffering must be exaggerated, but it must also be intelligible; and indeed, as Barthes shows, particular notions of intelligibility and of justice are the major factors which separate wrestling from boxing and make it the grandiloquent and fundamentally reassuring spectacle that it is.

The investigation of popular culture leads to the construction of a system which is the model of a cultural competence, but the categories and distinctions responsible for observed meanings are often less interesting than the semiological procedures by which conventional meanings are made to seem natural and inevitable. For an area in which the system itself is complex and fascinating—more so than the procedures the society devises to rationalize and obscure the conventions which produce meanings—one must turn to literature, where structuralism finds its most intricate objects and engages in its most frustrating if intriguing projects.

One might begin by distinguishing between a criticism that discovers structures or patterns of organization in literary works—for there is nothing novel in that enterprise—and a structuralism based on the analogy with linguistics, which considers literature as a system of signs. The latter is interested in formulating the conventions and assumptions which enable literary works to have meaning. That these are many and extremely important is not a difficult proposition to accept. If we imagine someone who knows English but has no knowledge of literature or acquaintance with the concept, we can well believe that he would be quite bemused if presented with a poem. He would understand individual phrases, certainly, but he would quite literally not know what to make of this strange linguistic construction. He would be unable to read or appreciate it as literature, because he would lack the complex system of implicit knowledge which a long literary experience affords. A structuralist poetics asks what is the nature of this knowledge, these codes and conventions, that must be postulated to account for our ability to read and understand literary works.

The best explicit statement of this programme comes in Barthes's *Critique et vérité.* Distinguishing between a criticism which attempts to assign meanings to works, and a 'science' of literature or 'poetics', he argues that the latter must be a study of the conditions of meaning: 'elle ne *donnera*, ni même ne *retrouvera* aucun sens, mais décrira selon quelle logique les sens sont engendrés d'une manière qui puisse être *acceptée* par la logique symbolique des hommes, tout comme les phrases de la langue française sont *acceptées* par le 'sentiment linguistique' des Français.'[16] Poetics attempts to reconstruct the general rules which make a range of meanings possible. The fact that a literary work may be given a variety of acceptable interpretations but that, at the same time, it cannot mean just anything at all, is the source of an elementary but crucial presumption: that by virtue of the logic of reading a work has a formal structure or a 'sens vide' which can be filled in various ways and which acts as a constitutive constraint on possible interpretations. Interested in the play of meaning, 'les variations de sens engendrées, et, si l'on peut dire, *engendrables* par les œuvres', poetics takes as its object not the various 'sens pleins de l'œuvre, mais au contraire le sens vide qui les supporte tous'.[17]

A single example will indicate the kind of factors involved. In *Seven Types of Ambiguity* William Empson cites a fragment of a translation from the Chinese:

> Swiftly the years, beyond recall.
> Solemn the stillness of this spring morning.

He observes that

> these lines are what we should normally call poetry only by virtue of their compactness; two statements are made as if they were connected, and the reader is forced to consider their relations for himself. The reason why these facts should have been selected for a poem is left for him to invent; he will invent a variety of reasons and order them in his own mind. This, I think, is the essential fact about the poetical use of language.[18]

Reading poetry is a process of producing meaning: one must invent something and this is possible only because one has assimilated a number of formal rules or procedures which guide invention and impose limits on it. In this case, the most obvious and strongest convention is what one might call the intent at totality of the interpretive process: poems are supposed to cohere, and one's exegetic labour must be directed towards that end. One must therefore discover a thematic level at which the two statements can be related to one another. What are some of the constraints which the text imposes on this process of invention? First, the contrast between 'swiftly' and 'stillness' provides the most obvious point of contact, and hence any interpretation should try to make thematic capital of this opposition. Secondly, 'years' in the first sentence and 'this morning' in the second, both located on the dimension of time, offer by way of opposition another connection; the reader might hope to find an interpretation which relates these two pairs of contrasts. This initial hypothesis about constraints seems to depend upon a formal principle, developed through one's experience of reading poetry, which makes the binary opposition a basic form of poetic organization: in interpreting a poem one looks for terms which can be placed on a single thematic or semantic axis but contrasted with one another.

These constraints suggest that one ought to try to relate the opposition between 'swiftly' and 'stillness' to different ways of thinking about time. Then one should be able to draw some thematic conclusions from the (unresolved) tension created by setting the two sentences against one another. This seems eminently possible: on the one hand, taking a large panoramic view, we can think of the human life-span as the unit of time and of years as passing swiftly; on the other, taking the unit as the moment of consciousness, we can think of the difficulty of experiencing time except discontinuously, so that every moment is, in a sense, outside of time. 'Swiftly the years' implies a vantage point from which one can consider time as movement, and the anxiety born of the swiftness of passage is compensated for by what Empson calls the 'answering stability of self-knowledge' derived from this panoramic view of life. 'This morning' implies other mornings—a discontinuity of experience implicit in the ability to name—and hence an instability which makes the stillness the more valued. This process of binary structuring, then, can lead one to develop not only a contrast between the two lines but also a tension within each of the lines which, as a common problem, serves to unite them. And since another of our conventions requires us to relate thematic contrasts to opposing values, we must think seriously about the advantages and disadvantages of these approaches to time. Naturally, a variety of conclusions are possible. The claim is not, in any case, that competent readers will agree on an interpretation but only that certain expectations about poetry and common structuring procedures guide the interpretive process and impose severe constraints on the set of 'acceptable' or plausible readings.

This example raises several important methodological points. First of all, it should be clear that the real object of poetics is not the work itself but its intelligibility. One must attempt to explain how it is that works can be understood; the implicit knowledge, the conventions that enable readers to make sense of them, must be formulated. But that does not mean—and this is the second point—that poetics must become a psychological or sociological discipline. One is not trying to explain the thoughts and feelings that arise in the mind of any particular individual, nor is one concerned with the statistical frequency and transitional probability of interpretations, as determined by sociological surveys, for, as in linguistics, the object of inquiry is competence rather than performance. One must begin with a range of interpretations which seem acceptable to skilled readers—otherwise one's theory will be simply irrelevant—but so long as this condition is fulfilled it does not matter how interpretations are gathered. One then attempts to determine, in a formal way, what norms and operations would have to be postulated to explain these results. The danger of such a study becoming excessively subjective is no serious problem, for, as Empson himself notes, the analyst must 'convince the reader he knows what he is talking about'—that the facts he presumes to explain are valid—and must 'coax the reader into seeing that the cause he names does, in fact, produce the effect which is experienced, otherwise they will not seem to have anything to do with each other'.[19] If he succeeds in this, then fears of impressionism will have been effectively calmed. The reader's acceptance of the explanation confirms that the effects proposed were valid.

The linguist confronts an analogous situation. There is no automatic procedure for establishing the facts to be explained, and surveys would be of little use, for he does not care whether speakers spontaneously recognize the ambiguity of *Flying planes can be dangerous*: that ambiguity is a fact of English because speakers will recognize and accept it when it is pointed out. Similarly, in poetics the analyst is less interested in what individual readers might happen to think upon first encounter with a poem than in what their literary competence leads them to accept as plausible when it is explained to them.

But however questionable the procedures of poetics might seem, there is really no viable alternative. Either the process of interpretation is random and idiosyncratic, or else it is governed by general norms and conventions. To claim that there is no system of interpersonal procedures to investigate would be to undermine the possibility of criticism itself, for—and there should be no mistake about this—every literary critic who is unwilling to present his work as a purely personal and arbitrary response to a text encounters the problems which poetics investigates. The possibility of critical argument, of ever convincing another reader that one's view of a particular text is a valid one, depends upon there being some shared point of departure and certain common notions of how one reads. The critic must invariably make decisions about what he can take for granted, what he must explicitly defend, and how a plausible or acceptable defence can be constructed. In so doing he depends on an intuitive sense of the nature of literary competence.

If investigation of the conventions which make literary communication possible be the approach suggested by the linguistic model, it is obvious that much of the work by self-proclaimed structuralists is, in Barthes's terms, criticism rather than structuralist poetics. Jakobson's studies of the distribution of various linguistic elements in poems, Todorov's isolation of formal structures shared by many of Henry James's short stories, Barthes's sketch of the psychological oppositions that can be used to organize the theatre of Racine, are all instances of a criticism intent on the discovery of structure but are not themselves major contributions to structuralist poetics, though they may apply some of its general principles.[20] They are distinguished from other critical studies by the novelty of some of their categories but primarily by their intense desire to systematize. Poetics is better represented by studies of narration, plot structure, and *vraisemblance* undertaken in recent years, of which the best example is Barthes's *S/Z*.[21] In that work one of Balzac's short stories is 'deconstructed' in considerable detail and the various 'codes' which readers use in organizing and interpreting its elements are identified and analysed.

*S/Z* is still very much a preliminary work, but it has the signal virtue of making clear, through its own failures of explanation, the complexity of the process of reading and the difficulty of accounting for even the most obvious facts about literary interpretation. How do we determine which actions are the main components of the plot, for it is clear that we do so? What makes some actions background information, realistic detail, devices of characterization? Under what conditions can we read something as a symbol and what determines our interpretation of it? How do we recognize irony? Questions such as these are basic to the study of literature and they should, in principle, receive an answer. After all, schools and universities have long presumed to offer literary training, to make students more competent readers; this creates a strong presumption that there is something to be learned. And if teachers are unable as yet to state what it is that they teach, they are quite confident of their ability to judge their students' progress towards literary competence. If they can recognize mastery, it should be possible to give some account of it.

The task will be a complex one, certainly; but the linguistic model would lead us to expect that. Though every child learns his native language we are still very far from being able to say exactly what rules he has mastered. The value of the linguistic model is to suggest that analogous tasks in other fields are theoretically possible, though difficult. One should at least attempt to make explicit the conventions which govern the production of meaning. In this sense a linguistically based structuralism is not simply the study of structures but the study of structures revealed by the analysis of systems of signs. And though many practitioners might well reject this view of structuralism, it has one considerable advantage: it unites in a single enterprise a series of fascinating projects, each fundamental to a particular discipline, and it does so through a model which encourages research by making clear the theoretical possibility of some very challenging tasks.

NOTES

1. 'Science versus Literature', *TLS*, 28 Sept. 1967, p. 897.
2. *Le Conflit des interprétations* (Seuil, Paris, 1969), p. 80.
3. 'Particular actions of individuals are never symbolic in themselves; they are the elements out of which a symbolic system, which must be collective, is constructed.' In 'Introduction à l'œuvre de Marcel Mauss', *Sociologie et anthropologie* (P.U.F., Paris, 1950), p. xvi.
4. See F. de Saussure, *Cours de linguistique générale*, 3rd ed. (Payot, Paris, 1967), pp. 100–1.
5. N. Trubetzkoy, *Principes de phonologie*, tr. J. Cantineau (Klincksieck, Paris, 1949), pp. 11–12: 'Phonology should investigate which phonic differences are linked, in the language under consideration, with differences of meaning, how these differentiating elements or *marks* are related to one another, and according to what rules they combine to form words and phrases.'
6. 'Some Controversial Questions in Phonological Theory', *Journal of Linguistics*, i. 2 (1965), 103.
7. *Purity and Danger* (Penguin, Harmondsworth, 1970), p. 48.
8. Ibid., p. 204.
9. Ibid., p. 54.
10. Ibid., p. 69.

11. Ibid., p. 70.
12. *Leçon inaugurale*, Collège de France, 5 Jan. 1960 (Gallimard, Paris, 1960), p. 11.
13. 'To look for the meaning of something is to discover what it resembles.' M. Foucault, *Les Mots et les choses* (Gallimard, Paris, 1966), p. 44.
14. 'When we say that cat and dog resemble one another less than do two greyhounds, even if the former are both tame or embalmed, . . . what is the ground on which we are able to establish this classification with such confidence? In what table, in what quality space of identities, similarities, analogies, have we become accustomed to distribute so many different and similar things? What is this coherence—which, as we can immediately see, is neither determined by an *a priori* and necessary deduction, nor imposed on us by immediately perceptible qualities?' Ibid., p. 11.
15. *Mythologies*, 2nd ed. (Seuil, Paris, 1970), pp. 13–24.
16. 'It will not present or even discover meanings, but will explain according to what logic meanings are engendered so as to be accepted by man's logic of symbols, just as sentences of French are accepted by the linguistic intuitions of Frenchmen.' R. Barthes, *Critique et vérité* (Seuil, Paris, 1966), p. 63.
17. '. . . the various meanings engendered or, as it were, capable of being engendered by works, . . . not the various "full" meanings of the work but rather the "empty" meaning which supports them all'. Ibid., p. 57.
18. *Seven Types of Ambiguity* (Penguin, Harmondsworth, 1961), p. 25.
19. Ibid., p. 249.
20. For Jakobson, see '*Les Chats* de Charles Baudelaire', *L'Homme*, ii. 1 (1962), 5–21; 'Une Microscopie du dernier *Spleen* dans *Les Fleurs du mal*', *Tel Quel*, xxix (1967), 12–24; *Shakespeare's Verbal Art in 'Th' Expence of Spirit'* (Mouton, The Hague, 1970). For Todorov's work on Henry James, see Chapter 5 below. For Barthes, see *Sur Racine* (Seuil, Paris, 1965).
21. *S/Z* (Seuil, Paris, 1970). For further discussion and an extensive bibliography, see my *Structuralist Poetics* (Routledge & Kegan Paul, London, 1973).

# 3 *Structuralism in Social Anthropology*

EDMUND LEACH

*Even the most enthusiastic adherent of structuralism in social anthropology will admit that the relationship between Lévi-Strauss's theoretical ideas and the empirical ethnographic facts in which they are said to be exemplified is very complicated. Summary examples can illustrate what is meant when it is argued that structuralism is, essentially, a 'way of looking at things', but they are unlikely to convince the sceptic that this is a means for arriving at the truth. At the end of the lecture, which is printed below, I endeavoured to give the listener a taste of the 'new' insights which can be derived from an application of structuralist procedures by offering an extremely condensed analysis of certain very familiar materials from the New Testament. I hope that no reader of this printed version of my lecture will imagine that the argument presented in this truncated form could persuade any serious Biblical scholar. I intend, in due course, to publish elsewhere a much fuller and more scholarly analysis on the same lines which will give the experts a better opportunity to assess both the merits and the limitations of such devices.*

STRUCTURALISM is a current intellectual fashion and the word itself has come to mean different things to different people, but for present purposes I shall assume that 'Structuralism in Social Anthropology' refers to the social anthropology of Lévi-Strauss and work which derives more or less directly from that source. Thus regarded, structuralism is neither a theory nor a method but 'a way of looking at things'. To see what is peculiar about this way of looking at things we may usefully look at some of the alternatives.

The subject-matter of social anthropology is customary behaviour. In every sequence of such behaviour there is a practical component which 'alters the state of the world' and a ritual, or symbolic, component which 'says something' about the social situation. For example, when you take breakfast in the morning, the practical aspect relieves your state of hunger but the nature of the food—whether it be 'toast and coffee' or 'bacon and eggs'—'says' that this is breakfast and not lunch or dinner.

In the history of social anthropology the bias of interest has lain alternately on one side or the other: Frazer, Durkheim, Radcliffe-Brown, Mauss, and Lévi-Strauss have been mainly concerned with 'things said'; Malinowski and his followers with 'things done'. The former have neglected economics and the latter have neglected religion.

Another recurrent uncertainty in social anthropology turns on the relationship between sociology and psychology. Are we concerned with social facts which are out there, external to man in the way that physical inorganic nature is external to man, or must we always remind ourselves that cultural products are *phenomena*, in the sense that they are not merely the perceptions of human minds but the products of human minds? And tied up with this is the question of whether we are ultimately concerned with the diversity of human nature or with its universals.

For if there *are* cultural *universals* then these are part of the 'nature of man'. They are products of 'the human mind' in a quite general sense, as distinct from any particular individual mind.

Frazer and Malinowski in their different ways both supposed that the study of social anthropology can lead to general insights about 'the human mind', whereas the 'collective consciousness' discussed by Durkheim and his associates was presumed to be a characteristic of particular societies. The metaphysics of such arguments are complicated and most British social anthropologists have wisely preferred to concentrate on the sociological part of the Durkheimian tradition—namely the thesis that society is an articulated system which exists in its own right independently of the individuals who make it up.

In this respect, as successors to Durkheim, Malinowski and Radcliffe-Brown both emphasized this articulated interdependence of the institutions which make up a social system. But where Radcliffe-Brown thought of the resulting society as a self-sustaining *organism* and proposed a taxonomy of such organisms, classified as species types, Malinowski thought of culture as a kind of ecological interface between the individual and his social and economic environment. For Malinowski, institutions serve to satisfy the *biological* needs of the individual; for Radcliffe-Brown they satisfy the *mechanical* needs of the *social system as such.*

Lévi-Strauss (by developing ideas initiated by Mauss) has attempted a synthesis of these two positions. The Durkheim–Radcliffe-Brown metaphor by which the articulation of *society* is seen as 'like that of an organism' is replaced in Lévi-Strauss by the proposition that the articulation of culture is 'like that of a language'. The superficial details of this language are peculiar to particular social systems; the way it is manipulated is the outcome of individual self-interest; but the ultimate grammar of the language is a human universal. But now to the matter in hand.

At the risk of repeating, or even contradicting, what Professor Lyons said, let me try to give you a rough—and it must be very rough—indication of where the interests of linguistics and social anthropology overlap.

By and large, social anthropologists prefer to leave the facts of human physiology to the physical anthropologists and the zoologists. This permits them to describe a vast area of human behaviour relating to food, sex, reproduction, respiration, body maintenance, and so on as 'natural'. All human beings are assumed to have roughly the same physiological needs and the same physiological responses. Behaviour which is the immediate undecorated outcome of these physiological drives—e.g. breathing, sleeping, eating, drinking, defecating, and so on—is looked upon as part of human *nature*. The residual category of 'non-natural behaviour' (in this blanket sense) is then treated as either *idiosyncratic*—peculiar to a particular individual—or *cultural*—peculiar to a group of human beings who have been brought up in a particular historical tradition.

In this approach, the capability of human children to learn to speak is a part of their *nature*. But particular languages which are mutually unintelligible are *cultural*. Members of a speech community use their spoken language to communicate information to one another. But they also use many other things to achieve the same purpose. The clothes we wear, the food we eat, the houses we live in, and so on, all convey information to those who understand the 'codes' in question. Structuralist social anthropologists start off with the hypothesis that these codes are 'languages' in the same sense (or very nearly the same sense) as spoken languages, and hence they postulate that the kind of linkage between nature and culture that has lately been emerging from the work of structural linguists is highly relevant for social anthropology.

Linguists have long recognized that although human languages are enormously varied in their superficial aspects, nevertheless there are principles which are valid for all languages. At one time, these universal principles were thought to be grammatical but from the end of the eighteenth century right through to about 1950 professional linguistic attention concentrated heavily on phonology. The experts attempted to formulate rules which would explain how one language could evolve out of another by regular sound shifts and, more generally, they sought to formulate rules about how noise elements (phonemes) can be distinguished from one another so that, when strung together in chains, they form distinctive words.

Since 1953, under the lead of Noam Chomsky, there has been a dramatic shift back to the study of grammar—the attempt to discover universal rules governing the construction of meaningful utterances.

It is important that you should appreciate that, in so far as structuralist social anthropology depends upon a borrowing of ideas from the linguists, these ideas come mainly from the theory of comparative *phonology* rather than from the general theory of *transformational grammar*. This may be a pity, yet it is so.

Anyway, just as structural linguistics endeavours to establish that there are 'deep level' universals which lie at the back of the diversity of human languages, so also structuralist social anthropology seeks to discover 'deep level' universals which lie at the back of the diversity of human cultures. Anthropologists have been searching for such universals for over 100 years with very little success. The structuralists think that they now have the key to the problem.

At this point I must explain the special sense in which I am using the word structure. By way of illustration I shall borrow an example from Bertrand Russell. If I listen to a broadcast version of a piano sonata the music has gone through a whole series of transformations. It started out as a score written on a piece of paper; it was interpreted in the head of the pianist and then expressed by movements of the pianist's fingers; the piano then produced a patterned noise imposed on the air which was converted by electronic mechanisms into grooves on a gramophone record; subsequently other electronic devices converted the music into radio frequency vibrations and after a further series of transformations it eventually reached my ears as patterned noise. Now it is perfectly clear that *something* must be common to all the forms through which the music has passed. It is that common something, a patterning of internally organized relationships which I refer to by the word *structure*. It is the very essence of structures (in this sense) that they are capable of expression in multiple forms which are transformations of one another, and further—and this point is often overlooked by practitioners of the structuralist art—that there is no one particular form which is a *more* true or *more* correct expression of the underlying structure than any other.

The notion of structure, thus defined, is a mathematical idea and empirical structures can be recognized in every aspect of the universe —in the physics of outer space just as in the genetic chemistry of molecular biology—but in linguistics and in social anthropology we are only concerned with the special class of structures which are generated by human brains. They have the peculiarity that the surface manifestations of these structures tend to be non-repetitive. New forms are being created all the time.

Structural social anthropologists, like structural linguists, are concerned to explore the mechanisms of communication between conscious human beings but they take a wider view of what constitutes communication. To start with they observe that we have receptor senses of taste, smell, touch, rhythm, sensuality, and so on, besides those of hearing and sight.

The social anthropologist therefore assumes that cultural forms which exploit these non-auditory, non-visual senses may function as instruments of communication *in essentially the same way* as the highly specialized cultural forms which we discuss under the heading of spoken and written verbal language.

Social anthropologists agree that it is language rather than any other special capacity which sharply distinguishes human beings from other primates. But in saying this they are using the word *language* in a rather unusual sense. All animals—including man—communicate with each other by means of complex stimulus-response mechanisms. There are some behaviourist psychologists of the school of B. F. Skinner who have managed to convince themselves that ordinary human speech is itself a mechanism of this sort. The linguists, however—and here I am referring especially to Chomsky—have argued with great vigour that human speech interchanges are wholly *unlike* stimulus-response mechanisms.

Although human speech behaviour is governed by discoverable grammatical rules, the way a sequence of verbal utterances will develop is no more predictable than the moves in a multidimensional game of chess.

In this debate, social anthropologists are on Chomsky's side. The interesting parts of cultural intercommunication do not depend upon stimulus-response mechanisms; they are linguistic in nature—generated within a context of grammatical rules—but the language involved is at least partly 'non-verbal'. When two individuals are in face-to-face communication 'the messages which are conveyed by words' and 'the messages which are conveyed by other means' are interwoven.

It is possible that the grammatical and phonological structures which can be incorporated in spoken language are more complicated than those which can be built into non-verbal forms of communication—though this is not self-evident—and I should not want to argue that the whole of structural linguistics can be incorporated *en bloc* into social anthropology by an adroit use of algebra and a switch of terminology. But it is suggested, very seriously, that any normal human being, when wide awake in the company of other human beings, is all the time receiving and conveying messages along a variety of different channels—the vocal/auditory channel being just one of many. The receiver of these messages is all the time integrating the information he is receiving through his different senses and attributing a single integrated meaning to his experience. He does not normally attribute one meaning to what he sees and something else to what he hears and something else again to what he touches . . . he fits the messages together into a single whole. It seems to follow that this integrating capacity of the brain (or 'mind' if you like) must be 'structural'. If we recognize that we exist in one world rather than many, it must be because we can recognize that messages that reach us through different senses simultaneously share a common structure.

But that is viewing matters from the receiving end. The individual who experiences multiple messages from outside as a unity is also a transmitter of messages through many channels. It is at least a plausible hypothesis that the messages which are sent out are just as structurally coherent as those which are taken in.

I have already cited the example of an English breakfast, and food behaviour in general illustrates the structuralist thesis very well. When we sit down in company for a formal meal we do not just scrabble for the nearest food available; everything is done in accordance with cultural conventions . . . Although the menu may not be known in advance the individual dishes have been prepared in a special and complicated fashion; they follow one another in predictable order and in predictable combinations. Certainly it is not immediately 'obvious' that the patterning of kinds and combinations of food, of modes of food preparation, of regulated sequences, etc. is 'the same as' the harmonic and melodic structure of a sheet of music, or the phonological and grammatical structure of a speech utterance, but once this analogic possibility is suggested, it is seen to be plausible. Structuralist social anthropologists go much further and say that it is so.

At this point the interests of the structural linguist and structuralist social anthropologist begin to diverge rather fast.

Orthodox experts in structural linguistics are not greatly concerned with *meaning* as such. Linguistics seeks to discover how it is possible at all for patterned sound to 'convey meaning' and, to this end, linguists are extremely interested in the fact that we are able to distinguish meaningful sentences from apparently similar meaning*less* sentences . . . for example, even a small child can recognize that 'the cat sat on the mat' and 'the gnat sat on the cat' are similar forms both of which make sense. Yet a very small phonetic shift which changes the second of these sentences into 'the mat sat on the cat' turns it into nonsense. How does this come about? Evidently our perception of meaning here depends on factors other than sound; this particular example seems to imply a deep-level classification system which distinguishes animate from inanimate objects and the relation of such classes to types of verbs.

But this kind of problem—the analysis of how sentences come to have meaning—is different from the problem of worrying about just what sentences mean. Specialists in linguistics do not ordinarily concern themselves either with problems of philosophy or with the task of translating foreign languages.

But the structuralist social anthropologist cannot split up theory and practice in this way. If he claims that the arrangement of cultural objects in space and of cultural objects in time is 'structurally organized' and that these 'structures' serve to convey meaning 'like' a grammatically organized spoken language, then he must not only show that the patterns in question exist; he must show what they mean. And that is not easy.

I should add here that I myself consider that a good deal of structuralist social anthropology, both in this country and in France, fails at just this point. The authors exhibit the existence of patterns in the material which they are examining, but they fail to demonstrate that the patterns are significant or how they are significant.

However, ignoring that point, how does the structuralist social anthropologist set about his task?

An analogy which has been used very frequently, particularly by Lévi-Strauss, is that of the music produced by an orchestra. The performers in an orchestra play different instruments; the musical score for each instrument is separate from that of any other instrument, so there is a sense in which each performer is providing a separate 'message'; but what is being communicated by the orchestra as a whole is a unity. The individual messages of the separate instruments only 'make sense' when they are combined as a whole. The individual messages (or, if you like, part-messages) provided by the individual instruments are like incomplete phrases or sentences in a speech utterance.

In conventional Western music (of the kind with which we are familiar in the works of Mozart and Beethoven) most of the phrases are melodic and the meaning of the sound elements is generated by sequence and contiguity. This of course is what happens in speech utterance also; the sound element, as represented by the letters of the alphabet, do not have meanings in themselves, they acquire meaning only when they are ordered in sequences to form words and sentences.

When structuralists refer to this process in which information elements acquire meaning *by contiguous association in sequence*, they are liable to talk about 'syntagmatic chains'. The jargon is horrible, but there it is. One important aspect of syntagmatic chains is that they are vehicles for the use of metonymy. That I am afraid is another jargon word though you will find it in the dictionary. Metonymy is the device whereby a part of a thing is made to stand for a whole. 'A' stands for Apple, 'C' for Cat, a Crown stands for a King, a Mitre for a Bishop, and so on. Musical melodies have this quality, the first few bars of a piece of music may serve to recall all the rest.

Shifting our frame of reference altogether, metonymy is what happens when 'meaning' is evoked as a signal by a stimulus-response mechanism. We can recognize metonymic messages only when they relate to very familiar highly conventional stereotyped patterns.

But to go back to the music of an orchestra. Each player has a score relating to his own particular instrument; the conductor has a score which combines *all* the instruments, and he reads it not merely from left to right, as a melodic or syntagmatic chain, but also up and down as harmony. The conductor generates musical meaning by getting the individual instruments to produce different noises simultaneously. It is the combination of this chorded dimension with the melodic dimension which produces the 'music as a whole'.

In speech utterances, metaphor plays the part of harmonic (chorded) association in music. Metaphor is the stuff of poetry; its power to stir the imagination and generate 'meaning' depends upon its unexpectedness and the chains of implied metonymic associations, which are unstated, and optional to the listener.

Just to be difficult, the structuralists, who refer to melodic sequences as syntagmatic chains, refer to the kind of shift of register which occurs in metaphor and harmony as 'paradigmatic'.

I think I have said enough now for you to see how the convinced structuralist approaches his data. He assumes that the cultural stuff within his field of observation, which consists of man-made things and customary behaviours, is all conveying information 'like an orchestra'. That being so, he assumes that it is possible to record the significant patterns in this cultural stuff on some kind of multi-dimensional orchestral score. As with orchestral music proper, the 'meaning' that is conveyed by the totality of cultural stuff results from a combination of two major types of association: (i) association by contiguity and sequence, melody, syntagmatic chains of data, (ii) association by metaphoric analogy, harmony, switches from one line of the score to quite a different line of the score, paradigmatic links of perceived similarity, e.g. 'My love is like a rose.'

And let me repeat again: there is a *major* difference between these two kinds of association. With syntagmatic chains you can set up rules which will distinguish between meaningful and non-meaningful combinations, for example in normal English, 'if a combination of three letters c.a.t. is to make sense, the letter *t* must come at the end.' But if I resort to metaphor I am asserting that $x = y$ and the number of entities which can be represented by either $x$ or $y$ is infinite and subject only to the control of my private imagination. I must emphasize that we are always using both modes of communication all the time, but the mix keeps changing.

But it is high time that I tried to show how this abstract theorizing may be applied to the normal subject-matter of social anthropology.

When I myself started out as an anthropologist as a pupil of

Malinowski the fashion was to emphasize that cultural materials must satisfy biological needs. Human beings cannot survive as individuals; they survive as members of communities, knit together by bonds of reciprocal obligation. To be viable, the cultural systems which generate these networks of interdependence must satisfy the biological requirements of the constituent members, notably those of food, sex, and shelter. Malinowski's style of anthropological thinking is now very unfashionable but its links with structuralism are closer than some of my colleagues seem to appreciate.

Ordinary spoken language is superimposed on a physiological essential, namely breath. In a comparable way the other major codes of human communication are superimposed on other physiological essentials, namely Malinowski's 'primary needs' of food, sex, and shelter.

I have already twice mentioned the case of food. All of us must eat, but under normal social conditions no human beings just eat indiscriminately. Cultural rules prescribe a classification which distinguishes between food and not-food. Other cultural rules specify how food shall be collected and prepared and how and when it shall be eaten. In every cultural system there is a 'grammar' of food behaviour which is as complex and specific as the grammar of speech.

This is equally true of sexual behaviour. Just as there is cultural discrimination between what is food and what is not food, so also there is cultural discrimination between what is sexually permitted and what is sexually forbidden. These are distinctions of culture and not of nature; they result from rules and conventions, not from inborn animal instincts.

In point of fact, the ordering of these two frames of reference—food and sex—is so similar that metaphoric cross-reference from one to another is almost universal. Even the details of the metaphors are repeated over and over again, e.g. sexual intercourse is 'like' eating; parturition is 'like' vomiting, and so on.

The fact that such symbolization occurs has been long recognized; it was the original basis for most psycho-analytic theorizing concerning dream interpretation and verbal free association. But the structuralist view of the process seems to be a good deal more sophisticated than that propounded by either Freud or Jung, or even Melanie Klein.

The structuralist proposition is that, in any one cultural system, the structure of ideas which relate to food is coherent by itself;

similarly the structure of ideas relating to sex is coherent; likewise the structure of ideas relating to space and orientation or, for that matter, the structure of ideas relating to interpersonal relationship—submission and dominance, respect and familiarity, and so on.

But the human brain which generates these coherent sub-systems is itself a unity; hence the structural coherence which is generated in the products of human brains, whether it is manifested as speech behaviour, or food behaviour, or sex behaviour, or whatever, must be general and mathematical. Metaphorical cross-reference becomes possible and appropriate only because the 'structure' is common. Each mode of communication is a transformation of each of the others, as in my example of the music on the gramophone record.

I shall try to give you some examples of how this theory can be applied to empirical anthropological data in a few moments but first let me go back to the source of these ideas—structural linguistics.

Structural linguistics started out as an explanation of phonology. Sound elements such as those we represent by the letters of the alphabet have no meaning in themselves; they acquire meaning only when they are strung together in chains. But how does the human brain distinguish between one sound element and another? Structuralist theory maintains that what we discriminate are not the sound elements (phonemes) as such, but the distinctive features which underlie the sound elements, such distinctions as vowel/consonant, compact high-energy sound/diffuse low-energy sound. These distinctions are, in effect, second-order data, 'relations between relations'. One merit claimed for this theory is that a small number of distinctive features may account for all the observable sound elements used in all natural languages. If this were true then distinctive feature theory ought to make it feasible to explore the possibility of language universals in a systematic way.

It is this 'distinctive feature' version of transformational phonology which has been mainly exploited by Lévi-Strauss in his application of structuralist ideas to social anthropology.

Lévi-Strauss's selection of culturally significant binary oppositions, the equivalents of vowel/consonant, compact/diffuse oppositions in phonology, often seems rather arbitrary but they fit with the ethnographic data surprisingly well. Here are some of them:

I. *Left hand* versus *right hand*. Every human individual is aware of the difference between his left hand and his right. He cannot describe with any precision what the difference is; one hand is, in fact, a complex, topological, transformation of the other. My two hands are alike in being hands; opposite in being left and right. This provides us with a useful basis of metaphor, and it was long ago observed that the usage which makes '*left*=sinister, evil, clumsy, mysterious' as opposed to '*right*=correct, good, and so on' is very widespread and not confined to any language area. Structuralism provides us with a clue as to why this should be so.

II. *Raw* versus *cooked.* Human beings characteristically eat part of their food cooked. The use of fire for cooking is what distinguishes men from beasts. Lévi-Strauss has argued that the worry about what it is that distinguishes true men—'people like us'—from mere beasts is an anxiety shared by all humanity everywhere. If this is true, then concern with the opposition Culture/Nature is basic even when the concepts as such do not exist. Lévi-Strauss postulates that *Raw* versus *Cooked* is a universal metaphor for *Nature* versus *Culture*. The opposition *wild* versus *tame* is very similar.

III. Spatial opposition. Structuralists find significance in such binary pairs as: Earth/Sky // Earth/Underground; This side of the river// The other side; Land // Sea; Dry // Wet; The City // The Desert. The point about such oppositions is that they are aspects of the non-living world external to man which present themselves directly to the senses but which are particularly appropriate for the crucial *social* opposition Us/Other. Of especial significance are those category pairs which can serve as a metaphoric bridge for the distinction between Culture and Nature since these serve as crucial pivots for religious thinking. In particular, 'Life/Death' becomes transferred by metaphor to 'This World/Other World' and to 'Man versus God'.

IV. *Sister* versus *Wife* (see Fig. 1). If we accept the proposition that a sister can never be a wife, then *x*/*y* forms a binary dyad and the social relationship A/C (+) will always be in some sense opposite to B/C (−). If we then observe how these two relations A/C and B/C are expressed in customary behaviour we shall get a guide as to the coding involved. For example in some cultural systems A/C=blood (common substance) and B/C=metaphysical influence. This allows us to predict that when A/C=metaphysical influence, then B/C=Common substance. On the whole, empirical ethnography confirms this expectation.

But what, you may well ask, is the point of all this? Well first of all it is characteristic of this kind of argument that it is assumed that the elements of symbolism are not things in themselves but 'relations' organized in pairs and sets. Let me give an example. Fifty years ago in the first flush of Freudian enthusiasm it was seriously argued that it is universally the case that elongated objects are treated as penis

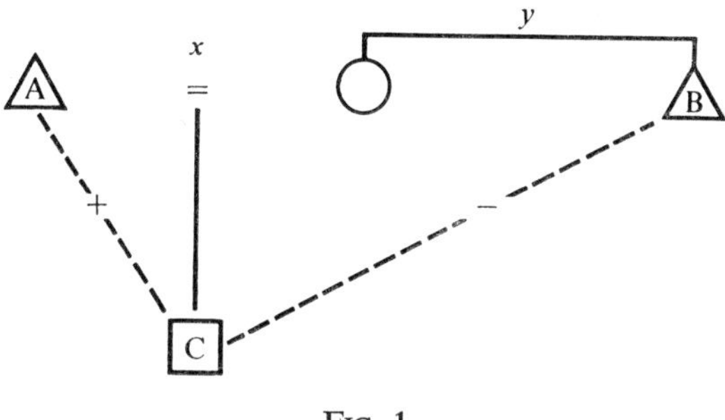


FIG. 1

symbols, while oval and circular objects serve as vagina symbols. The structuralist admits that there is substantial ethnographic evidence for this kind of generalization but makes the interpretation more abstract. The category opposition long/round is part of a much more general structure (Fig. 2).

A. *For simple-minded Freudians*

long object = penis
round object = vagina

B. *For structuralists*

$$X = \frac{\bigcirc}{|} \text{ or } \frac{+}{-} \text{ or } \frac{\bigcirc}{\triangle} \text{ or } \frac{\text{round}}{\text{straight}} \text{ or } \frac{\text{female}}{\text{male}} \text{ or } \frac{\text{vagina}}{\text{penis}}$$

FIG. 2

The crucial point is that the 'element of structure' is not a unit *thing* but a relation *X*.

Applied to ethnographic data this more abstract approach encourages the social anthropologist to perceive that cultural phenomena which he had previously thought of as quite separate are really variations of a common theme.

It is difficult to exemplify this point in detail to a partly non-anthropological audience but here is an example. The fact that some human societies trace descent through the mother and others through the father has been known for centuries. In the mid-nineteenth century this became a central pivot of evolutionary thought. It was argued that since the child's connection with its mother is 'more obvious' than its link with its father, therefore matriliny is more primitive than patriliny. Hence matrilineal societies and patrilineal societies came to be thought of as entities of quite different kinds but no one really bothered to think about just *how* they were different.

According to this traditional classification the Kachins of north Burma are a patrilineal society. The Garo of Assam, who are located about 100 miles further west, are a matrilineal society. Both groups have been known to Western ethnographers for over a century. Both are distinguished by what appear to be rather peculiar

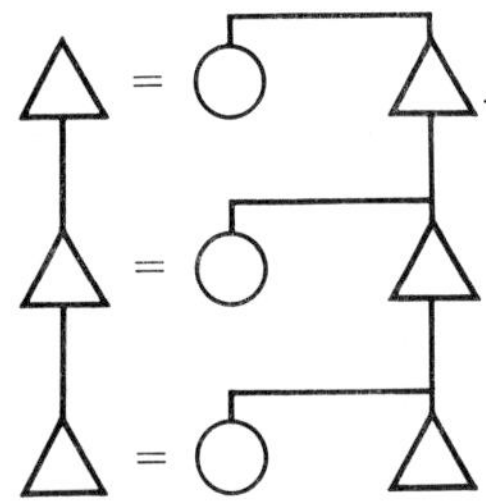

*Kachin schema*
'marriage with the mother's brother's daughter'

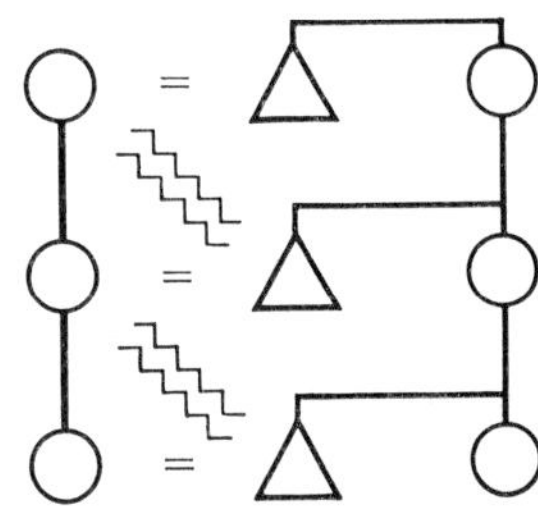

*Garo schema*
'marriage with the mother-in-law'

FIG. 3

marriage rules. Garo men were reputed to marry their mothers-in-law; Kachins allegedly always married their mother's brother's daughter. No one before Lévi-Strauss ever detected any similarity between the two systems.

But a structuralist way of looking at things shows that these two marriage rules are versions of the same principle (Fig. 3), and modern fieldwork has shown that the two cultural systems are in fact remarkably similar right across the board. The contrast patrilineal descent/matrilineal descent being the only major difference between them. A structuralist therefore regards the two systems as transformations of a single structure.

The 'variation on a theme' argument is also the key characteristic of the structuralist analysis of mythology which is the aspect of

Lévi-Strauss's work which looms largest in bulk (if not in quality) in the total Lévi-Straussian corpus.

In this field the essential innovation in Lévi-Strauss's approach is the recognition that mythological stories always exist as sets rather than isolates. The individual members of the set constitute permutations of the same theme. The moral implication of the mythology, what Malinowski called its force as 'a charter for social action', can only be fully apprehended when we take the total set of stories into consideration simultaneously. Once again you need to think of the instruments of an orchestra combining to produce a unitary piece of music.

Lévi-Strauss's theory of myth takes up four very fat volumes of closely argued text. To give a 'summary' of that argument seems to me almost impossible. What I propose to do instead is to illustrate the argument by applying it, in very cursory form, to a theme from the New Testament of the Christian Bible. But first some points of general theory about the relationship between mythology and moral precept.

Among human beings, as among other animals, the three primary drives governing the interaction of individuals are hunger, sex, and physical aggression. Among species *other than* man these drives are very largely determined by genetic factors, or by conditioning at a very early stage in the individual's development. As I have already emphasized, in man the rules and conventions which determine with whom we may eat and what we may eat, with whom we may sleep and where we may sleep, whom we may assault with impunity and under what circumstances, are all arbitrary, culturally determined matters. Taken together, these rules and conventions serve to carve up the social environment into a vast array of cross-cutting classes of things and persons in terms of which we organize our daily lives. The tidy ordering of these categories is something to which we all attach great importance. Any infringement of the standard conventions generates a sense of emotional shock which we experience *either* as embarrassment *or* as excitement.

And even in a story, any reference to a transgression of taboo, however oblique, creates vicarious excitement. In this respect the myths of our own society have quite a different quality for *us* from the myths of other people. Myths everywhere make constant reference to moral offences, but unless, as listener or reader, you share the same moral assumptions as the myth narrator, you will not be 'shocked' by what he says and you will then have difficulty in picking up the message. For it is the *shock* effect of references to breaches of moral taboo which gives myth its 'meaning'. That is why the myths which are most widely recognized as powerful and exciting are ones which harp on themes of a very basic moral kind, themes which crop up in all kinds of cultures and not just as local peculiarities.

These *primary* myths are always centrally preoccupied with persons and creatures who are wrongly constructed or wrongly born or in the wrong place, and with such universal moral offences as homicide, sexual misdemeanours, and abnormal food behaviour. Such myths exhibit the limits of normality and the potent dangers of otherness by turning normality back to front.

Men and animals are normally different, so, in myth, the serpent who is abnormally constructed, talks with Eve like a human being; normal boats float on the sea, so Noah's Ark comes to rest on the top of a mountain; parricide and incest are the ultimate sins, so myth tricks Oedipus into killing his own father and marrying his own mother. The moral point is made clear by emphasizing the overwhelming disasters which are directly associated with the mythical breach of normality.

Perhaps *normality* is not quite the right word. The topographical space in which mythical events take place is metaphysical rather than physical. It consists of 'the world of common experience', which is *normally* inhabited by normal men and by *tame* animals, *plus* 'the other world' of imagination which is *normally* inhabited by supernatural beings and *wild* animals. But there is also a very important 'intermediate world' which is neither here nor there. In myth it is this liminal zone which receives the greatest attention.

*Normality* and *abnormality* must therefore be viewed in context. Other world beings are 'abnormal' when they behave like normal beings of this world; normal men are 'abnormal' when they behave like gods; beings of the middle zone, who often appear in myth as deified ancestors (part man, part god), become 'abnormal' whenever they lose their ambiguity. The mediating hero is, in all religious systems, a being of the middle zone. One aspect of his essential ambiguity is that he (or she) is always, at one and the same time, impossibly virtuous and impossibly sinful; it is a definitional characteristic of the hero that he is 'abnormal when judged by ordinary criteria'.

There are dozens of familiar Biblical examples of this principle.

The myth makes Abraham marry his half-sister which is incest and it makes Solomon, the Great King, take seven hundred wives and three hundred concubines all from the nations with whom the Israelites were formally forbidden to intermarry. Notice how, on this issue of marriage, the stories of Abraham and Solomon form a contrasted pair. They are concerned with two aspects of the same problem, the *over*emphasis and the *under*emphasis of the same rule of endogamy. This is an example of what I mean when I say that myth stories do not occur as isolates but in sets; the message of the myth is made obliquely by repetitive, yet contrasted, references to the *same* moral injunction which is transgressed in *different* ways.

This sounds all very well in theory, but if I am to show *you* just how myth actually works by storing up emotional feelings of shock and contradiction so as to reveal a religious message, then I have to work through an actual example which you yourselves, or some of you anyway, are liable to find shocking. I must take a myth which is part of your *own* religious background. Hence my choice of Christian New Testament material. The theme which I propose to tackle is that which is implicit in the myth of the birth and death of the paired hero figures, John the Baptist and Jesus Christ.

First you should notice how although the gospels link the careers of these two heroes together in the most emphatic way, the heroes themselves are treated as opposites. In both cases, conception is abnormal, but where John's mother Elizabeth is a woman past the age of childbearing, Jesus' mother Mary is a virgin. Then again the two mothers are cousins, but whereas John belongs to the priestly line of Aaron, Jesus belongs to the royal line of David.

Let me elaborate further some of the structural transformations of this similarity–difference relationship. John is a prophet living in the wilderness, that is to say on the margins of this world and the other; he dresses in animals' skins and feeds off locusts and wild honey; he abstains from alcohol; his companions are wild animals; he is thus a man of *Nature*. Jesus is repeatedly declared to be a king; he lives on normal food in the normal world of the city; he is the son of a carpenter; he fraternizes with publicans and sinners; he is thus a man of *Culture*. Jesus submits to baptism by John yet at this instant John expresses verbally his subordination to Jesus.

Eventually John dies by *decapitation*. Throughout the Old Testament this is a death reserved for kings and princes. In contrast Jesus dies by crucifixion. This is an alien form of execution introduced by the Roman conquerors and reserved for criminals. John's death is brought about by the conspiracy of a wicked Princess Herodias and the sexual guile of her daughter Salome. The women around Jesus play an entirely virtuous sexual role, yet one of them, Mary Magdalene, has been a prostitute.

The context of John's death is a royal feast at which John's severed head is served up on a dish as if it were food. The context of Jesus' death is a Jewish feast of the Passover at which Jesus himself identifies his own body and blood with the food and wine.

I think you must agree that, when the stories are summarized in this selective way, the symmetry of the contrasted patterns is very striking. But what does it mean? We can get an answer to this question by extending the set of stories under examination. For example, we might notice that in the Jewish myth, the *original* Passover commemorated the liberation of *Israelites* from domination by the *Egyptians* and their escape through the *wilderness* to the *Promised Land of Canaan.*

In contrast, the Christian myth of the Last Supper, which is explicitly identified with the Jewish Passover, commemorates the liberation of all *Mankind* from domination by the *cares and suffering of ordinary worldly life*, and *Man*'s escape, through the *mysterious wilderness of death* to the *Promised Land of God's Heavenly kingdom and eternal life*. In the *Jewish* myth the final signal of release is the *divine* destruction of all the first born sons of the *Egyptian oppressors*. In the *Christian* myth the final signal of release is the *human* destruction of the first born son of *God*. Thus, the Christian story is, in a quite explicit sense, a new version of the much earlier Jewish story but generalized on to a more metaphysical plane with certain key elements reversed.

If you consider the material in this way you will realize that part at least of the 'message' in the New Testament story is that the symbolic heroes John and Jesus exchange their roles. John starts out as a being from the other world; he is 'filled with the Holy Ghost even from his mother's womb'; he is a 'voice crying in the wilderness'; but he dies in a city in a kingly palace, executed as a king.

Jesus starts out as a being of this world; he belongs initially to the city not the desert; his royal status is emphasized from the start but he becomes filled with the Holy Ghost only when he is baptized by John; he then immediately goes out into the wilderness, but when he does so he is in communication not with God but with Satan; nevertheless Jesus ends up as a being of the Other World. John is a prophet, a spokesman of God, who becomes a murdered king; Jesus is a king who becomes a murdered prophet.

This role reversal is reinforced by many other incidents in the Jesus myth which repeatedly reverses the roles which orthodox Jewish belief seems to offer to the Messiah. For example, where the ancient *Israelites* had escaped from *Pharaoh* by flight *from Egypt into Canaan*, the infant Jesus escapes from *Herod* by flight *from Canaan into Egypt*. When Jesus dies he is *not* in a palace but outside the city on a gibbet. He dies *not* as a king, but as a mock king, wearing a crown of thorns. Indeed he dies as a common criminal. Yet, by thus dying, he achieves the status which John had at the beginning; he forms a bridge with the other world and life everlasting.

The drama of the Christian mass, the communion service, recapitulates the myth of the Last Supper. The communicant, by identifying himself with Jesus through the food of the sacred meal, assures himself of life everlasting in the other world, but in doing so, he *also* identifies himself as a criminal and miserable sinner in this world. But the communicant also aspires to improving his personal spiritual status; he seeks to become on some spiritual plane more king-like. But does this mean more like Jesus or more like King Herod? The ambiguity of implication is quite typical of all mythological structures.

Notice that in the process of dramatization the historical context of the story becomes entirely irrelevant. It really does not matter in the least whether *any* of this 'actually happened in history'. The message of the myth is true in its own terms, not in historical terms.

I realize that such a web of references, cross-references, identifications, inversions, and transformations is difficult to follow. Indeed, if structuralists are right about how myth works, it is an essential feature of the matter that, at a conscious level, the logic of the transformations should be ambiguous. The message of the myth is full of paradox, and it only becomes acceptable as a religious injunction because we do *not* quite understand what is being said.

This is just as well because in this, as in all major myths, the literal sense of what is being said is very terrible. If we leave the metaphysics on one side, we are being told that, in order to achieve the God-like quality of immortality, we must first kill and eat God himself. But we miss the point if we try to constrain our material by imposing any such *literal* interpretation. As a German theologian has put it, 'Myth is the expression of unobservable realities in terms of observable phenomena.' Myth possesses an *inner* sense which underlies a superficial *non*-sense; we can understand it only as we might understand a kind of universalized poetry.

This I am afraid has been a rather crowded paper. Clearly my Biblical example, if it were to be fully justified, would need much greater elaboration. But I started out by saying that structuralism in social anthropology is a distinctive way of looking at things. I felt that I needed to exemplify this point. Whether, at the end of the day, we have or have not gained any insights which we did not have before will be a matter of opinion.

# 4 *Social Life as a Sign System*

UMBERTO ECO

I AM speaking to you. You are understanding me, because I am following the rules of a precise code (the English language), so precise that it also allows me to make use of it with a lot of phonetic and grammatical variations. Its strong underlying structure in some way acts like a loadstone which magnetizes and attracts my deviations from the norm. You understand me because there exists a code (a sort of inner competence shared by you and me) and there exist possible messages, performed as concrete utterances and interpretable as a set of propositions.

I am using signs. The code (the *langue*, according to Saussure) couples a sign-vehicle (the *signifiant*) with something called its meaning or its sense (the *signifié*), something to be better defined later. As a semiotic entity the sign is—according to Peirce[1]—'something which stands to somebody for something (else) in some respect or capacity'. Let us accept these two definitions as two unquestionable starting-points for the following discourse.

However, Peirce has said more: 'A sign is anything which determines something else (its *interpretant*) to refer to an object to which itself refers (its *object*) in the same way, the interpretant becoming in turn a sign, and so on ad infinitum.'[2] If the interpretant is not, as many so-called semioticists believe or sometimes believed, the interpreter, but if it is a sign which translates, makes clear, analyses, or substitutes a previous sign, then the world of semiosis proceeds from sign to sign *in infinitum regressum* (but is it *regressum* or *progressum*?). In this continuous movement semiosis transforms into signs everything it encounters. To communicate is to use the entire world as a semiotic apparatus. I believe that culture is that, and nothing else.

When I said that I was speaking to you, I meant that I was speaking by means of verbal devices, recognized and classified by linguistics. But I am also speaking (if you prefer, communicating) through my voice inflections. I am musically, or 'tonemically', using my voice in order to become persuasive, interrogative, provocative, shocking—in order to underline my attitudes, to emphasize my understatements or my paradoxes. Maybe I do not properly perform the tonemic code used by an English speaker: I should like to express irony, you detect a shadow of perplexity, or vice versa. I do not share completely the English *paralinguistic code*. Until a few years ago linguists maintained that they were not entitled to theorize concerning such types of behaviour as voice qualities, ranges, pitches, dispositions of accents, purely emotional interjections; for this reason they put all these features into a sort of no-man's-land, that of free variants and of idiosyncratic performances. Paralinguistics is now able (when possible) to systematize, and (always) to classify in repertoires this kind of behaviour.

I am speaking through my gestures. Not only as an Italian; from my point of view Anglo-Saxons also have a very articulated gestuality, as emphatic as the Latin one, maybe less conceived as a substitute for words and rather more intended to underline abstractions, but anyway a gesticulation subject to a complete theorization. A new branch of communication theory called *kinesics* deals with this important topic.

I am speaking through my facial expressions. I could state some important ideas, and yet I could underline them with calculated movements of my eyebrows, tongue in cheek, biting my lips, or with ironic smiles, which could subdue or destroy the conceptual force of my statements. Kinesics, again, deals with these forms of behaviour, and has proposed a complex and strongly organized kind of shorthand in order to note every significant feature of facial muscular movements.

I am speaking through my body position in respect to other bodies interacting in a given space. If I were speaking standing up instead of sitting, if I moved towards you, if I were walking among you instead of remaining hierarchically fixed in my place, the very sense of my words would be changed.

I am speaking through my collocation in a public space; I am connoting my discourse by the fact that I speak here and my audience is sitting in front of me, and we are not all sitting together around a table or co-involved in a revolutionary sit-in. You would agree with me that spatial forms in this room (in every building and town) are conceived in order to suggest, to induce types of behaviour. A new branch of semiotics, *proxemics*, assumes that this is not a matter of suggestion or mere stimulation, but that it is a process of signification, any spatial form being a precise conventional message conveying social meanings, on the basis of existing codes.

I am speaking through my clothes. If I were wearing a Mao suit, if I were without tie, the ideological connotations of my speech would be changed. Obviously fashion codes are less articulate, more subject to historical fluctuations than linguistic codes are. But a code is no less a code for the fact that it is weaker than other stronger ones. Gentlemen button their jackets, shirts, and coats from left to right, ladies from right to left. Suppose I were speaking of semiotics, standing in front of you, buttoned from right to left: it would be very difficult for you to eliminate a subtle connotation of effeminacy, in spite of my beard.

I could continue to list the various ways in which we are communicating and exchanging information. The fact is that communication neither has to do with verbal behaviour alone, nor involves our bodily performances alone; communication encompasses the whole of culture.

Several decades ago Ferdinand de Saussure composed a passage of his *Cours* that at that time was purely utopian and to many readers sounded rather paradoxical:

> La langue est un système de signes exprimant des idées et par là comparable à l'écriture, à l'alphabet des sourds-muets, aux rites symboliques, aux formes de politesse, aux signaux militaires, etc. etc. Elle est simplement le plus important de ces systèmes. On peut donc concevoir une science qui étudie la vie des signes au sein de la vie sociale. Elle formerait une partie de la psychologie sociale et par conséquent de la psychologie générale. Nous la nommerons sémiologie—du grec *semeion*, signe—Elle nous apprendrait en quoi consistent les signes, quelles lois les régissent. Puisqu'elle n'existe pas encore, on ne peut pas dire ce qu'elle sera. Mais elle a droit à l'existence, sa place est déterminée d'avance.[3]

Now let me quote another definition, given by C. S. Peirce, one of the founders of the semiotic discipline: 'I am, as far as I know, a pioneer, or rather a backwoodsman, in the work of clearing and opening up what I called semiotic, that is, the doctrine of the essential nature and fundamental varieties of possible semiosis.'[4] Peirce was the first to list the various possible kinds of signs. Among his various triadic classifications, there are an enormous number of proliferating ramifications ( I shall spare you them because I believe that their use during a lecture is not admitted by the Geneva Convention). Peirce listed:

(a) *symbols*—that is arbitrary devices such as the words of verbal language;
(b) *indexes*—that is either *symptoms,* natural events from which we can infer other events (for instance, the footprints which revealed to Robinson the presence of Friday on the island), or the so-called *deictic* signs, such as a finger pointed towards an object, or a pronoun or an adjective in the context of a phrase (for instance: 'Once upon a time there was a girl living in a forest. THAT girl was named Little Red Riding Hood.');
(c) *icons*—a very large category of signs supposed to possess some of the properties of their referent, which now are increasingly revealed to be less homogenous than common opinion believed, and are being submitted to an intensive criticism and to new attempts at description, classification, semiotic foundation.[5]

Peirce and Saussure were the first to foresee the existence of a new discipline, linked to linguistics only in so far as linguistics is the most developed communication science and entitled as such to furnish blueprints for any other approach. It is difficult to maintain that the entire set of linguistic categories can be applied to the other sign systems. The basic assertion which links semiotics to linguistics is only this: that all sign processes can be analysed in the same sense in which linguistics can, that is as a dialectic between codes and messages, *langue* and *parole*, competence and performance. The task of semiotics is to isolate different systems of signification, each of them ruled by specific norms, and to demonstrate that *there is* signification and that *there are* norms. Nevertheless semiotics aims to become able to describe, to structure, and to legitimate its entire field using a unified set of theoretical tools. To assert that semiotics is not a branch of linguistics does not mean that semiotics has neither autonomy nor unity. It may signify simply that linguistics is one of the branches of semiotics.

I cannot now explore the whole challenging and exciting landscape of these identities and differences. I can only limit myself to listing the different paths of research that semiotics foresees or actually recognizes as its own proper field: *zoosemiotics*, the study of *olfactory and tactile communication*, *culinary codes*, *medical semiotics* (becoming a branch of a general semiotics), *musical codes*, *formalized languages*, *secret alphabets*, *grammatology* (as the study of writing), *visual communications* in general, *graphic systems*, *iconic signs*, *iconography* and *iconology*, *card games*, *riddles*, *divination systems*, *systems of objects* and *architectural forms*, *plot structures*, *kinship structures*, *etiquette systems*, *rituals*, the *typology of cultures*, and so on, as far as the upper levels of *rhetorical systems* and *stylistic devices*.

The wish of Saussure seems now crowned with success. Semiotics covers the entire field of culture (or social life). But Saussure only wished to see a discipline able to study the life of signs 'au sein de la vie sociale'. He did not say—as semiotics today claims (and as the title of my lecture suggests)—that the whole of social life could be viewed as a sign process, or as a system of semiotic systems. The recognition of a great number of sign repertoires cannot convince one that those repertoires *are systems*, nor can we take for granted that any cultural phenomenon *is a sign*. Nevertheless, in order to adopt a semiotic approach one must assume that any cultural manifestation *can be viewed* as a communication process. The task of this lecture, then, will be neither to demonstrate the possibility of a general, complete, and satisfying formalization of the entire semiotic field, nor to demonstrate that any sign repertoire is necessarily a system. My purpose is more basic: I have, above all, to demonstrate that any cultural phenomenon is *also* a sign phenomenon.

Please note that I could propose two hypotheses. One of them is more radical, a sort of unnegotiable demand on the part of semiotics: that *the whole of culture must be studied as a phenomenon of communication*. Then there is a second more moderate hypothesis: *all aspects of a culture can be studied as the elements of content of communication*. Our first step will consist in the clarification of the second, moderate hypothesis. We shall see later that the acceptance of the second hypothesis implies the acceptance of the first.

Let me return to my first way of approach. I am speaking to you; you understand me because my messages are emitted following the rules of a commonly shared code. This code is not only the English language in so far as it makes a precise (or an ambiguous) denotative meaning correspond to every word; it is a complex set of subcodes, based on various cultural conventions, making understandable, for instance, some technical uses of terms—the fact (if you like) that in saying 'culture' I mean (and you understand) a particular anthropological notion of culture, and not the petit bourgeois conception of a remunerative collection of bookish items.

The code couples a repertoire of sign vehicles (the English vocabulary) with a repertoire of meanings. As we shall see later it is not a question of two repertoires, but of many systems. We can accept, as a starting-point, the very important subdivision proposed by Louis Hjelmslev:[6]

| | |
|---|---|
| | Substance |
| CONTENT | ------ |
| | Form |
| ------------- | |
| | Form |
| EXPRESSION | ------ |
| | Substance |

It is very easy to understand what the difference is between Form and Substance of Expression, but it is very hard to penetrate the difference between Form and Substance of Content.

Contemporary linguistics knows almost everything about the structure of the Form of Expression: phonetics, phonology, lexicology, grammar have investigated for many centuries (or for many decades) its complex articulation. On the contrary, we know very little about the Form of Content. The immense realm of the Form of Content was supposed, by many linguists, to be extraneous to the linguistic empire. It was conceived of as the proper and private matter of cultural anthropology, of physical science, studying the so-called 'properties' of things, or of philosophy, dealing with abstract ideas, concepts, values. The task of language seemed only to be that of conveying these non-linguistic contents. The task of linguistics seemed to be that of explaining how language units articulate in order to be uttered. The fact that they were able to express contents was accepted just as a matter of fact; the way in which they performed this process remained rather mysterious.

Saussure was the first to pose the problem without resolving it: a sign is not only a linguistic unit, or if you prefer, a linguistic unit is not only a sign vehicle. A sign results from the coupling of a *signifiant* and a *signifié*. After Hjelmslev linguistics has gone further: if language units are articulated into minor units (not only phonemes, but also morphemes and lexemes, in Martinet's sense) the task of linguistics is maybe to make a minimal semantic unit correspond to a minimal vehicular unit (a portion of *signifiant* to a portion of *signifié*). Hjelmslev suggested that, given four lexical units such as *ram*, *ewe*, *hog*, and *sow*, it is possible to reduce these units to intersecting combinations of four more general semantic properties not exclusively pertaining to them. Given two zoological marks such a 'porcine' and 'ovine' and two sexual marks such as 'masculine' and 'feminine' one can obtain the units I have listed by the simple articulation of these more general categories. 'Masculine' plus 'porcine' gives *hog*, and so on.[7]

You can easily understand that here we are facing a situation very akin to that of articulated language. We have a repertoire of semantic items, some of them corresponding to nouns, some to adjectives (though we do not analyse these distinctions today: they are all *semic* features), and of combinatorial rules allowing the birth of new, more complex items. All these elements are neither properties nor necessarily words, as we shall see later; they are simply semantic units. The rules governing them are still to be fully discovered, but their existence and the fact that they are probably submitted to a sort of articulatory discipline not so different from that of language—all this is irrefutably evident.

Before claiming that in this universe of semantic units there is a hierarchy (as there is in lexicology between nouns, adjectives, or prepositions); before maintaining that there is or there is not an exact correspondence term to term between the units of expression and content units (all these are problems that we cannot touch now), we have to make clear a fundamental point: what do we mean by a *semantic* or a *cultural unit*? What is its mode of existence?

Let us say that culture subdivides the entire range of human experiences (known and classified objects, abstract ideas, things and values, hopes and fears, tested material phenomena and logical connections, and so on) into systems of pertinent features. Let me give an example:

<table>
<tr><th>Latin</th><th>English</th></tr>
<tr><td rowspan="2">mus</td><td>mouse</td></tr>
<tr><td>rat</td></tr>
</table>

Modern English culture has made pertinent two semantic or cultural units (units of the Form of Content) cutting up that universe of Substance of Content which is pure raw experience, and in which ancient Latin civilization isolated one and only one more general unit. There are not only two words in English where Latin had only one; there are two 'things', I mean two sign vehicles conveying two meanings, two items from the system of the Form of Expression in order to express two items from the system of Form of Content.

It goes without saying that any one of these English items could be semantically (we prefer today to say semically) analysed by splitting it into at least two semic components: a mouse is a 'parvulus mus' and a rat is a 'mus magnus' (obviously there are other differences, other distinguishing features). As far as every one of these units might correspond (term to term or in some other more informal way) to an associated or to many associated units of the Form of Expression (which, we must remember, was sometimes for some currents of thought the only recognized object of linguistic science), the system of content comes under the control of semiotics. If a discipline called semiotics is possible, it *must* be concerned with the Form of Content.

This happens not merely because, as commonsense suggests, any cultural unit becomes the possible content of one or more units of expression. (In this reduced sense the supposed 'imperialism' of semiotics is less than apparent. Anybody agrees with the statement that British Rail, while organizing the transport of passengers, is concerned with human beings too. But British Rail is not a biological or anatomical institute; it knows passengers only as passengers.) When I make the assertion that semiotics is concerned with content, I am saying much more. I am saying that semiotics must deal with the inner constitution of cultural units in so far as they are ruled by semiotic laws. The first reason for this, and the one I wish to deal with now, is that cultural units, in so far as they are semantic units, are not only *objects* but also *means* of signification. In this sense they are encompassed by a general theory of signification. But this is exactly what we have to demonstrate.

Suppose we are reading a good English translation of the Bible. Suppose that we read that Jonah was swallowed by a big FISH (the Hebrew text says TAG). Some commentator discovered later that this fish was a dolphin, but common opinion and medieval tradition are both convinced that it was a WHALE. Suppose now we are reading a zoological treatise where whale is quoted as a mammal. And suppose we are reading Melville's *Moby Dick*. Melville suspected (and the text says it in Chapter 32) that a whale was a mammal. But he preferred to believe (and Ahab, Ismael, the entire crew of the *Pequod* strongly believed) that a whale was something like a BIG FISH. Melville explicitly refused the classification of Cuvier.

So there exist in this respect two semantic systems (deriving from two cultural contexts) and in reading one of our three texts we must always consider which system is implied. I mean by semantic system a particular field of the Form of Content—in this case the one concerned with animals, opposing in a very complex network of mutual relationships fishes, mammals, birds; ungulates and celenterates; aerial and terrestrial animals; and so on. Each system generates many more simple and local oppositions, called axes, such as the opposition *wild* versus *domestic*. (It is clear that from our standpoint systems are not previously given—they do not have a sort of ontological consistency—but are posited at the moment in which semiotics supposes a structure in order to render understandable a given set of performances.)

Moreover, whether the medieval system or the modern zoological one is implied, the same sign vehicle is always employed. Saussure should have said that there are two signs, but not because there are two *signifiants*: only because there are two *signifiés*. Thus, in three different occurrences the same sign vehicle means at least two cultural units. As a matter of fact some texts (and Melville's is amongst them) impose a sort of *double jeu*, asking the reader to shift from one system to another, in order to reach that ambiguity which is the main feature of a poetic text. For Melville a whale is neither a fish nor a mammal, but 'a big fish with warm bilocular heart, lungs and a "penem intrantem foeminam mammis lactantem"'.[8]

The last quotation shows that a sign vehicle constitutes the starting-point of a sort of semantic tree made by imaginary arrows branching into different positions in a number of semantic fields or axes—though obviously such an abstract representation of the semic components of a lexeme like 'whale' is the result of an oversimplification:

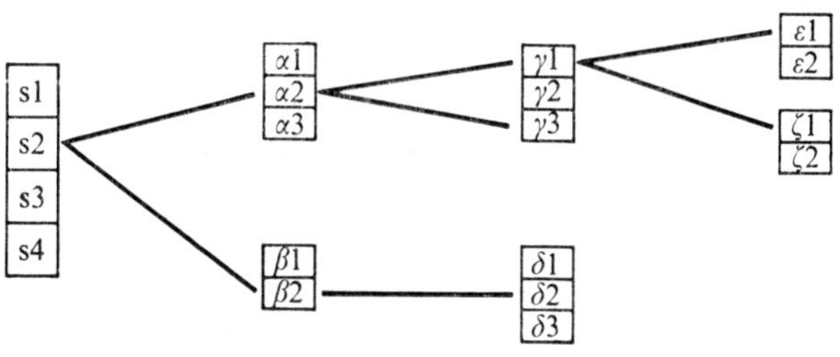

At this point let me make another step towards our theory of the semiotic nature of cultural units. Let us consider the use of the sign vehicle /whale/ within the convention establishing that a whale is a fish, a big fish 'living on the surface of the water, so long that the sand can cover it and transform it into an island' (I quote a definition from a medieval Latin Bestiary). This big fish, so cunningly able to cheat men in order to catch them, throughout the entire medieval Christian tradition connotes the Leviathan. The Leviathan connotes the Devil: the Biblical tradition of the Middle Ages considers the adventure of Jonah as a journey to Hell. When Melville uses the image of the whale he explicitly refers to these diabolical connotations: the whale is Evil. Melville has to make some rhetorical effort in order to convince his reader, but a medieval story teller (or sculptor) and his audience would have found themselves more at ease with this topic. The relationship whale–monster–Leviathan–Devil–Evil would have been clearly and explicitly fixed by those connotative subcodes called Bestiaries.

In this sense we discover that a cultural unit not only possesses a sort of systematic oppositional relationship with other cultural units pertaining to the same semantic field; it is also inserted into a sort of chain of continuous references to other units belonging to completely different semantic fields. The sign vehicle seems to be not only the beginning of a diagrammatically bidimensional tree, but it also appears as a sort of multidimensional topological construction in which the starting node and every node the tree touches generate other ramifications, each node referring back to a number of others, in a labirinthine interconnection of mutual definitions and mutual connotative implications. In other words a cultural unit is not only something which *stands against* something else, it is something which *stands for* something else. May I remind you that 'something standing for something else' is a sign?

Let us now resume the three relationships entertained by the sign *whale* (I mean by sign the sign vehicle plus its meaning; by meaning a cluster of semic components, a *sememe*; by sememe the active principle, the source of energy of chains of connotation). As A SIGN VEHICLE /whale/ denotes a cultural unit, the most conventional, such as is fixed by any dictionary. The process of denotation does not imply a further analysis of the given unit. The sign vehicle plunges (so to speak) into a precise position in a given semantic field, or in a precise semantic axis. The denotation of the sign vehicle /whale/ is that unit which is not a dolphin and which is not a shark (I continue to oversimplify). AS A CULTURAL UNIT denoted by the sign vehicle, 'whale' refers connotatively back to other units in different semantic fields: monster, Devil, Hell. But note that this kind of relationship does not belong to the sign vehicle /whale/ as an English word; the connotative relationship belongs to the semantic unit 'whale' which could be expressed just as well by the Latin word /cetus/ or the Italian word /balena/. A semiotic approach is not only concerned with verbal symbols but also with cultural units (*quod erat demonstrandum*). AS A SEMEME 'whale' plunges into different positions in several semantic fields, each of these positions becoming one of its semic components: a whale is a mammal, big, living on the surface of the sea, possessing a very useful fat stratum under the skin, warm-blooded, and so on. The entire complex of these semic components constitutes the sememe 'whale' (obviously in the medieval semantic system the components were different):

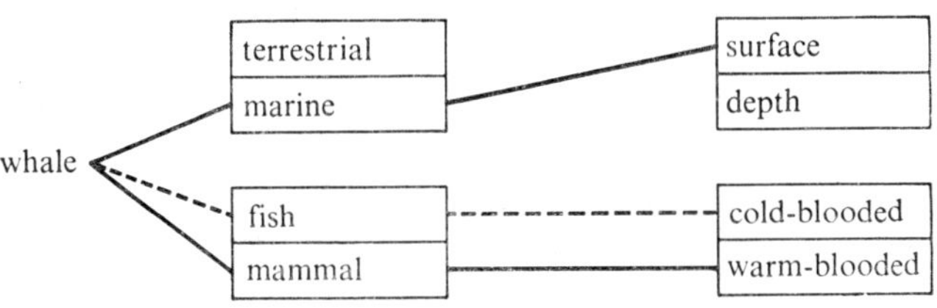


Now let us reconsider our tripartition. At first glance a cultural unit seems something like a thing, a concept, an idea. Unfortunately concepts and ideas (leaving aside such an elusive entity as a 'thing') are not so easily definable. However, we can define a cultural unit semiotically: it receives its collocation from the relationship it entertains with other items of the system.

I mean that, answering the question 'What does /wood/ mean?', we have two solutions. One of them is the componential analysis of the semic components of the sememe 'wood' (something very akin to a definition in terms of physical properties, except that a semic definition can conceive of contradictory semic properties, a physical one cannot). The other is the simple consideration of the space occupied in a semantic field by the unit 'wood' as compared to the apparently corresponding units of other parallel systems. Let us compare three little axes, in English, Italian, and German, following a classical example of Hjelmslev's:[9]

<table>
<tr><td>1</td><td rowspan="2">wood</td><td>legno</td><td>Holz</td><td>1</td></tr>
<tr><td>2</td><td>bosco</td><td rowspan="2">Wald</td><td>2</td></tr>
<tr><td>3</td><td>forest</td><td>foresta</td><td>3</td></tr>
</table>

Please forget that these notions have names and let me call them by numbers (referring to the graduated scale defining common spaces or positions in all the axes). In this way we are able to say that the denotative meaning of the English word /wood/ is the position 1–2. The meaning of the Italian word /bosco/ covers only position number 2. One could add that maybe the two cultural units corresponding to /legno/ and /bosco/ are also two in English culture, where the single word /wood/ seems to be only a case of homonymy. The English speaker distinguishes very well the wood of which his chair is made from the wood in which he is bird-watching. But I am not sure that the same happens with the German word /Wald/ to which correspond, in English and Italian, two words and two cultural units. For a German a small number of trees is only a 'kleine Wald' or a 'Wäldchen'.

Suppose now that in a precise cultural context there exists a connotative chain linking the sememe 'forest' with the complex significations 'human life' or 'sinner's journey through life', as is the case in Dante's *Divina commedia.* The allegorical sign vehicle of the meaning 'sinner's journey' is not any particular word, but principally position number 3 of our schema (independently of the word which conveys it and independently of the language—English, Italian, or Chinese—used). Only one problem arises: in some languages there could not exist a word signifying position number 3, because the cultural system in which that language works does not conceive of such an isolated cultural unit as position number 3 (any quantity of trees, from two to two thousand representing for its users a single cultural unit, without any difference between a garden with a hammock, a little wood, an immense tropical forest; or for the simple reason that the users do not know, from a geographical point of view, any ensemble of trees).

You have probably realized that during my lecture I have never cited such a deceptive entity as the referent (Frege called it *Bedeutung*). According to many students of semantics the referent is the actual object to which the sign vehicle corresponds. I have not time now to undertake a refutation of the referential fallacy (I did that in a paper published recently in *VS*)[10] but you can easily understand to what extent the notion of the real object corresponding to the sign is absolutely irrelevant to any semiotic purpose. It is entirely irrelevant to know if whales really exist or if Jonah was really swallowed by one, provided that the sign vehicle /whale/, and the statement /*Jonah was swallowed by a whale*/, was completely understandable to a Bible reader in the past as it is now. It is only because one can understand them that signs and statements act as social forces. A logician, in connection with the necessity of verifying a statement in terms of truth or falsity, may say that the term /transubstantiation/ has no extension, that is, no referent, and therefore has no meaning. But, from a semiotic standpoint we are compelled to recognize that the enormous amount of *intensions* the term has possessed have made it the cause of theological battles, military conflicts, social changes, hope and death, salvation and fear.

However, there is one way in which actual objects, which are useless for checking the semiotic value of a sign, enter again into the semiotic concern. Suppose that a medieval traveller (as Saint Brendan was), well acquainted with Bestiaries and the Biblical tradition, sailing on the North Sea suddenly saw a whale. This living object would immediately become to his eyes (and to his mind) something which *stands for* the Devil (or Hell, or Evil). The living *token* /whale/ is understood as a semiotic *type* signifying something else. It is a sign. Alanus ab Insulis wrote:

> Omnis mundi creatura—quasi liber et pictura—nobis est in speculum.
> Nostrae vitae, nostrae mortis—nostri status, nostrae sortis—fidele signaculum.

You cannot say that this situation is only typical of medieval civilization. Having lost the Bible as our leading cultural code we have acquired Thorstein Veblen, Vance Packard, or the world of advertising. Is our reaction in front of a Rolls-Royce, intended as a precise connotative sign meaning 'prosperity', 'power', or 'upper social status', so different from the medieval attitude? And when we get into a new model of sports car and are able to recognize and use the gears, what happens if not the sudden recognition of the possible function exactly denoted by the basically conventional form /gear lever/? A semiotics of objects as means of communication is possible because, as Barthes said,[11] in so far as there is a society, every function becomes in turn the sign of itself; and because not only the expressly intended communicative object, but every object may be viewed (and in fact is continually interpreted and used) as a communication device, as a sign.

When the first australopithecine used a stone for breaking the skull of a baboon, there was as yet no culture, even if presumably at this point the first technical tool was invented. Culture arises only when: (1) a thinking being establishes the new function of an object; (2) he names it as 'object *x* performing function *y*' (it is not necessary to name it to somebody, or to name it aloud—as Peirce said, ideas too are signs); (3) reviewing the same object he recognizes it the day after as the object named *x* performing the function *y* (it is not necessary for the human being to perform the function again).

These three conditions do not imply the existence of two human beings. They can also apply to Robinson alone on his island. The object, conventionally recognized as the vehicle of a possible function, transmits the information emitted by the Robinson of yesterday to the Robinson of today. When the individual becomes two, these two also need new substances of expression: they need words in order to transmit the meaning 'function *y*' without always carrying around the object itself, as the wise men of Laputa used to do. But the word is only a *new* sign for the *same* cultural unit, the function. It is also possible to show the object directly (as the sign of its function) and for the communication process still to take place.

This process is possible from the moment that culture exists. But culture exists only because this process is made possible. Culture presupposes the semiosic use of any one of its items: sounds, images, actual objects, bodies. If we read attentively the first book of *Das Kapital* by Karl Marx we shall see that an object, endowed with use value, in so far as it acquires an exchange value, becomes the sign vehicle of other objects. Marx not only shows how commodities, in the general framework of economic life, may become sign vehicles referring to other goods; he also shows that this relationship of mutual significance is possible because the commodity system is precisely a system, structured by means of oppositions, as semiotic systems are. It is only because a commodity acquires a position within the system that it is possible to establish a code of commodities, in which one semantic axis is made to correspond to another semantic axis, and the goods of the first axis become the sign vehicle for the goods of the second one, which become in turn their meaning. Marx indicates this process saying that commodities possess an exchange value IN WHICH is expressed the value of another commodity, the value OF WHICH is the meaning of the former. The relationship is reversible.

Similarly, at the level of the sign vehicles of verbal language, /automobile/ can be the significant form expressing the meaning /voiture/, or /whale/ can be the significant form expressing as its meaning the Hebrew equivalent /tâg/—these two relationships being equally reversible. Similarly in the process of signification, the sign vehicle /whale/ can be the significant form expressing a complex semantic unit subjected to many definitions, but the entire set of these definitions may in turn be understood as the organized expression of a lexical content which is the word /whale/. Similarly the presence of a real /whale/ may be understood as the significant form referring back to a sememic unit, or maybe to the lexical entry /whale/.

C. S. Peirce defined the sign as 'anything which determines something else (its *interpretant*) to refer to an object to which itself refers . . . in the same way, the interpretant becoming in turn a sign, and so on ad infinitum'.[12] The interpretant is another sign (or something assumed as a sign) which explains or translates, or substitutes, the first sign, in order to make the world of unlimited semiosis progress, in a sort of spiral movement, actual objects never being touched as such, but always transformed into significant forms. This process of unlimited semiosis is the result of the humanization of the world by culture. In culture any entity becomes a semiotic phenomenon. The laws of communication are the laws of culture. Culture can be studied completely under a semiotic profile. Semiotics is a discipline which must be concerned with the whole of social life.

NOTES

1. C. S. Peirce, *Collected Papers* (Harvard University Press, Cambridge, Mass., 1931–5), ii. 228.
2. Ibid., ii. 303.
3. F. de Saussure, *Cours de linguistique générale* (Payot, Paris, 1960), iii. 3.
4. C. S. Peirce, *Collected Papers*, v. 488.
5. Cf. Umberto Eco, *La Structure absente* (Mercure de France, Paris, 1972), section B; 'Introduction to a Semiotics of Iconic Codes', *VS-Quaderni di studi semiotici*, ii (1972) (and the whole of issues ii and iii,

with several articles on this topic); *Communications*, xv (1970) (special issue on 'L'analyse des images').

6. *Prolegomena to a Theory of Language* (University of Wisconsin, Madison, Wis., 1961), ch. 13, pp. 47 ff.
7. Ibid., ch. 14, p. 70.
8. Chapter 32.
9. See *Prolegomena*, ch. 13, and 'Pour une sémantique structurale', in *Essais linguistiques* (Nordisk Sprog-og Kulturforlag, Copenhagen, 1959).
10. U. Eco, 'A Semiotic Approach to Semantics', in *VS*, i (1971).
11. R. Barthes, 'Éléments de sémiologie', in *Communications*, iv (1964), II.1.4.
12. C. S. Peirce, *Collected Papers*, ii. 303; cf. W. Wykoff, 'Semiosis ad Infinite Regressus', in *Semiotica*, ii. 1 (1970).

# 5 *The Structural Analysis of Literature: the Tales of Henry James*

TZVETAN TODOROV

*Essays on the subject of Structuralism and literature have without doubt appeared in far greater quantity than those pieces of actual structural analysis that have been produced. This combination of terms was created—and condemned—long before anyone was imprudent enough to venture along such a dangerous road. It has thus almost been forgotten that there exist means of making structural analysis known other than by meditating upon its (im)-possibility: by practising it. I have chosen this means in preference, taking as my material the tales of Henry James, and, for a theoretical discussion of the subject, I take the liberty of referring the reader to other texts which have appeared in the last few years.*[1]

*As we embark upon this analysis, however, there is one precaution which we must not forget. 'Structuralist criticism' is a contradiction in terms: criticism seeks to interpret a particular work, while Structuralism, for its part, is a scientific method implying an interest in impersonal laws and forms, of which existing objects are only the realizations. The structural analysis of literature is nothing other than literary theory; however, the latter's objective is not the interpretation of works, nor is there a 'structuralist' interpretation that is better as such than other methods—exegesis is to be assessed according to its coherence, not according to its truth in an absolute sense. The fact is, then, that these two forms of activity, the hermeneutic and the scientific, need as much to be distinguished as to be put into contact with each other. Literary theory (poetics) provides criticism with instruments; yet criticism does not content itself with applying them in a servile fashion, but transforms them through the contact with new material. It is in order to profit from this continual two-way movement that I have adopted my present course. In illustrating the structural analysis of literature by the interpretation of a particular text, all that I can aim at is a mould-like image—the excuse for which must be that it thus renders homage to the object of this study: Henry James.*[2]

IN his famous story *The Figure in the Carpet* (1896)[3] James tells how a young critic who has just written an article on one of the authors, Hugh Vereker, he most admires, happens to meet him shortly afterwards. The author does not hide from him the fact that he is disappointed with the study dedicated to him. It is not that it lacks subtlety; but it fails to name the secret of his work, a secret which constitutes at the same time its motive principle and its general meaning.

> There's an idea in my work [Vereker explains] without which I wouldn't have given a straw for the whole job. It's the finest, fullest intention of the lot, and the application of it has been, I think, a triumph of patience, of ingenuity . . . It stretches, this little trick of mine, from book to book, and everything else, comparatively, plays over the surface of it (pp. 281–2).

Pressed by his young interlocutor's questions ('Can't you give a fellow a clue?') Vereker adds: 'My whole lucid effort gives him the clue—every page and line and letter. The thing's as concrete there as a bird in a cage, a bait on a hook, a piece of cheese in a mouse-trap . . . It governs every line, it chooses every word, it dots every i, it places every comma' (pp. 283–4).

The young critic throws himself into a desperate search. Seeing Vereker again, he tries to obtain more precise information: 'It was something, I guessed, in the primal plan, something like a complex figure in a Persian carpet. He highly approved of this image when I used it, and he used another himself. "It's the very string", he said, "that my pearls are strung on"' (p. 289).

In approaching Henry James's work, let us take up Vereker's challenge (Vereker said, after all: 'So it's naturally the thing for the critic to look for. It strikes me . . . even as the thing for the critic to find' (p. 282)). Let us try to find the figure in Henry James's carpet, the primal plan on which everything else depends, as it appears in each one of his works.

The search for such an invariant factor can only be carried out, as the characters of *The Figure in the Carpet* well know, by superimposing the different works one on the other, like Galton's photographs, reading them as if they were a series of transparencies. However, I have no desire to make the reader impatient, and shall reveal the secret immediately, even if I run the risk thereby of being less convincing. In this way the works I shall examine will, I hope, confirm my hypothesis, instead of leaving to the reader the trouble of formulating it for himself.

James's tales are based on the quest for an absolute and absent cause. Let me explain one by one the terms of this formula. There exists a cause—to be understood in a very broad sense. It is often a character, but sometimes also an event or an object. Its effect is the tale, the story which we are told. The cause is absolute: everything in the story owes its presence, in the last analysis, to it. But it is absent and we set off in quest of it. And it is not only absent but for most of the time unknown as well; only its existence, not its nature, is suspected. There is a quest: that is, the story consists in the search for, the pursuit of this initial cause, this primary essence. The story stops if it is found. On the one hand then, there is an absence (of the cause, of the essence, of the truth) but this absence determines everything; on the other hand, there is a presence (of the quest) which is simply the pursuit of the absence. The secret of James's tales is, therefore, precisely this existence of an essential secret, of something which is not named, of an absent, overwhelming force which puts the whole present machinery of the narrative into motion. The movement of James's stories is a double and, in appearance, a contradictory one (which allows him to start it ceaselessly over and over again): on the one hand he deploys all his strength to reach the hidden essence, to unveil the secret object; on the other, he constantly moves it further and further away. He protects it up to the end of the story, if not beyond. The absence of the cause (or of the truth) is present in the text; still more, it is its logical origin, its *raison d'être*; the cause is that which, by its absence, gives rise to the text. The essential element is absent; absence is an essential element.

Before illustrating the many variations of this 'figure in the carpet', I must deal with a possible objection: that not all of James's works follow this same pattern. Even limiting ourselves to the tales alone, we find some which do not share this movement, though it is present in most of them. Two further explanations are therefore necessary. The first is that this 'figure' is tied more especially to one period in James's life: it dominates his work almost exclusively from 1892 until at least 1903, when James was in his fifties. During these twelve years James wrote almost half his tales. Those written before this period can only be considered, in the light of this hypothesis, as work of a preparatory nature, brilliant, but not original, exercises, which fall within the framework of the lesson James learnt from Flaubert and Maupassant. The second explanation is of a theoretical, not a historical order: it may be supposed, it seems to me, that an author approaches this 'figure in the carpet', which resumes and underlies the whole of his writing, more closely in some of his works than in others. And this explains the fact that, even after 1892, James continued to write tales that belong among his 'realistic' exercises.

Let us begin with the most elementary case: that in which the story is formed around a character or a phenomenon surrounded by an aura of mystery which is lifted at the end. *Sir Dominick Ferrand* (1892)[4] can be taken as an example of this type. It is the story of a poor writer, Peter Baron, who lives in the same house as a musical widow, Mrs. Ryves. One day Baron buys an old desk; and, by the greatest of chances, he discovers it to have a double back and therefore a secret drawer. Baron is fascinated by this first mystery, and succeeds in penetrating it: he takes a few bundles of old letters out of the drawer. An unexpected visit from Mrs. Ryves—with whom he is secretly in love—interrupts his exploration; she has had an intuition that Peter is threatened by some danger, and, noticing the bundles of letters, begs him never to look at them. This sudden action creates two new mysteries: what is the content of the letters? how can Mrs. Ryves have had such an intuition? The first of these is resolved a few pages later: the letters contain compromising information about Sir Dominick Ferrand, a statesman who died several years beforehand. But the second mystery persists until the end of the novel, and its explanation is delayed by other repercussions. These concern Peter Baron's hesitation as to what to do with the letters. He is approached by the editor of a magazine, to whom he has revealed their existence, and who offers him a considerable sum for them. Each time he is tempted (he is extremely poor) to make the letters public, a new 'intuition' of Mrs. Ryves's, with whom he is falling more and more in love, arrives to stop him. It is this second force that wins the day, and in the end, Peter burns the compromising letters. The final revelation follows: Mrs. Ryves confesses to him, in an outburst of sincerity, that she is the illegitimate daughter of Sir Dominick Ferrand, the child of the same liaison as the letters are about.

Behind this vaudeville-like plot—with characters turning out in the end to be close relatives of one another—one can discern the fundamental scheme of James's tales: the absolute and secret cause of all the events is an absent factor (Sir Dominick Ferrand) and a mystery (the relationship between him and Mrs. Ryves). The whole of her strange behaviour is founded (with hints of the supernatural) on this secret relationship, and her behaviour, moreover, determines Baron's. The intermediary mysteries (what is in the desk? what are the letters about?) are other causes which, because they are unknown, provoke the presence of the tale. The appearance of the cause brings the tale to an end; once the mystery has been uncovered, there is nothing else to tell. The presence of the truth is possible, but it is incompatible with the tale.

*In the Cage* (1898)[5] is another step in the same direction. Ignorance, here, is not due to a secret which could be revealed at the end of the story, but to the imperfection of our means of knowledge; and the 'truth' which is arrived at in the final pages is, in contrast with the certain and definitive truth of *Sir Dominick Ferrand*, nothing else but a lesser degree of ignorance. This lack of knowledge is caused by the profession of the principal character and by the centre of her interests: the young lady whose name we never learn is a telegraphist, and all her attention is directed towards two persons whom she only knows through their telegrams: Captain Everard and Lady Bradeen.

The young telegraphist possesses hardly any information concerning the lives of the two people that interest her. In fact she only has three telegrams, around which she builds up her hypotheses. The first is this: 'Everard, Hôtel Brighton, Paris. Only understand and believe. 22nd to 26th, and certainly 8th and 9th. Perhaps others. Come. Mary' (p. 145). The second: 'Miss Dolman, Parade Lodge, Parade Terrace, Dover. Let him instantly know right one, Hôtel de France, Ostend. Make it seven nine four nine six one. Wire me alternative Burfield's' (p. 181). And the last: 'Absolutely necessary to see you. Take last train Victoria if you can catch it. If not, earliest morning, and answer me direct either way' (p. 219). On this meagre canvas the telegraphist embroiders a whole romance in her imagination. The absolute cause here is the life of Everard and Lady Bradeen; but the telegraphist knows nothing of it, shut up as she is in her cage at the post-and-telegraph-office. Her quest is thus all the longer, all the more difficult, and, at the same time, all the more exciting.

The only meeting that she has with Everard outside the post-office —between the second and the third telegrams—sheds little light on his character. She can see what he looks like physically, observe his gestures, listen to his voice, but his 'essence' remains as intangible as it was when they were separated by the glass cage, and possibly more so. The senses perceive only what is secondary—appearances. They cannot reach as far as the truth. The only revelation (but we dare not call it that) comes at the end, in a conversation between the telegraphist and her friend Mrs. Jordan. This lady's husband, Mr.

Drake, has been engaged by Lady Bradeen; so Mrs. Jordan is able to help her friend, though only slightly, to understand what has happened to Lady Bradeen and Captain Everard. Her understanding is made particularly difficult, however, by the fact that she pretends to know much more than she actually does, so as not to be humiliated in front of her friend; her ambiguous replies prevent certain revelations from being made. 'Why, don't you know the scandal?' Mrs. Jordan asks, to which her friend answers evasively: 'Oh, there was nothing public.' One must not, however, overestimate the extent of Mrs. Jordan's knowledge; in answer to her friend's further questions she explains:

> 'Why, he was *in* something.'
> Her comrade wondered. 'In what?'
> 'I don't know. Something bad. As I tell you, something was found' (pp. 239–40).

There is no truth; there is no certainty. All we are left with at the end is this 'something bad'. Once the story is finished we cannot say we know who Captain Everard was; we are simply less ignorant than we were at the beginning. The essence has not made itself present.

When, in *The Figure in the Carpet*, the young critic was searching for Vereker's secret, he asked the following question: '"Is it something in the style or something in the thought? An element of form or an element of feeling?" He indulgently shook my hand again, and I felt my questions to be crude and my distinctions pitiful' (p. 284). Vereker's condescension is understandable. Were we to be asked the same question about the figure in Henry James's carpet, we should have just as much difficulty in finding a reply. Every aspect of the story shares the same movement, as we shall try to prove.

Critics have frequently pointed out (as James himself did) a 'technical' feature of these tales: every event is described from someone's point of view.[6] We learn the truth about Sir Dominick Ferrand not directly, but through the eyes of Peter Baron; in fact as readers we never see anything but Baron's consciousness. The same is true of *In the Cage*: the narrator never at any moment places before the eyes of the reader the experiences of Everard and Lady Bradeen, but only presents him with the telegraphist's picture of these experiences. An omniscient narrator could have named the essence, but the girl is not capable of doing so.

James cherished this indirect 'vision' above everything else—'that magnificent and masterly indirectness',[7] as he calls it in a letter—and carried the exploration of it to considerable lengths. He describes his work thus: 'I must add indeed that, such as they were [the Moreens, characters in *The Pupil*], or as they may at present incoherently appear, I don't pretend really to have "done" them; all I have given in "The Pupil" is little Morgan's troubled vision of them as reflected in the vision, also troubled enough, of his devoted friend.'[8] We do not see the Moreens directly, we see X's perception of the perception of Y, who sees them. An even more complex case appears at the end of *In the Cage*: we observe the telegraphist's perception of Mrs. Jordan's perception, and she in turn tells what she extracted from Mr. Drake who, in *his* turn, only knows Captain Everard and Lady Bradeen from a distance.

Speaking of himself in the third person, James continues: 'Addicted to seeing "through"—one thing through another, accordingly, and still other things through that—he takes, too greedily perhaps, on any errand, as many things as possible by the way' (p. xviii). Or, as the narrator of *The Beldonald Holbein* says: 'It is not my fault if I am so put together as often to find more life in situations obscure and subject to interpretation than in the gross rattle of the foreground.'[9] It is not surprising, therefore, that we only see the 'vision' of a character, and never, directly, the object of this 'vision'; nor is it surprising to find in James's writings sentences like this: 'He knew I really couldn't help him and that I knew he knew I couldn't.'[10]

But this 'technique', about which so much has been written, of 'visions', or points of view, is no more a 'technique' than, let us say, the themes of the text. We now see that James's indirect 'vision' is a part of the same 'figure in the carpet' as we discovered in our analysis of the plots of his stories. The fact that he never gives a clear and full representation of the object of perception, the cause of all the characters' efforts, is nothing but a translation into another form of the general theme of the tales: the quest for an absolute and absent cause. The 'technical' elements of these works have the same significance, therefore, as the thematic, and these, in turn, are as 'technical' (that is to say, organized) as the rest.

What is the origin of this idea of James's? In a sense all he has done is to erect his method as a narrator into a philosophical concept. There are, basically, two ways of depicting character. Here is an example of the first:

This dark-skinned, broad-shouldered priest, condemned hitherto to the austere chastity of the cloister, shivered and burned alternately at this night-scene of love and passion. The sight of this lovely, dishevelled girl in the arms of a young and ardent lover turned the blood in his veins to molten lead. He felt an extraordinary commotion within him; his eye penetrated with lascivious jealousy under all these unfastened clasps and laces (Victor Hugo, *Notre-Dame de Paris*).[11]

And here is an example of the second:

She noted that his nails were longer than was the custom in Yonville. Looking after them was one of the clerk's principal occupations; and he kept a special knife for this purpose in his desk (Flaubert, *Madame Bovary*).[12]

In the first case the character's feelings are directly described (in our example the direct character of the narrative is attenuated by rhetorical figures). In the second, the essence is not named. On the one hand it is presented to us through someone's vision of it; on the other, the description of the features of a character's personality is replaced by that of an isolated habit—the famous 'art of the detail', in which the part replaces the whole, following the well-known rhetorical figure of synecdoche.

For some time James followed in Flaubert's wake. When we spoke of his earlier 'exercises' we were referring to those texts, precisely, in which he carries his use of synecdoche to perfection, and one can find examples of the same tendency right up to the end of his life. But in the stories with which we are concerned, James has gone one step further: he has become aware of Flaubert's sensationalism (or anti-essentialism), and instead of using it simply as a means, he makes it the constructive principle of his work. All that we can see is appearances, and their interpretation remains doubtful; only the quest for truth can be present; truth itself, although the cause of this movement, remains absent (as, for instance, in *In the Cage*).[13]

Let us now take another 'technical' element: composition. What does the classic short story, for instance Boccaccio's, consist in? If we approach it at a fairly general level we could say that, at its most simple, it tells of the passage from a state of equilibrium or disequilibrium to another such similar state.[14] In the *Decameron* it is often the conjugal ties of the two protagonists that constitute this initial equilibrium, which is then upset by the infidelity of the wife. A second state of disequilibrium appears at a second level at the end: the two lovers escape the punishment threatened by the deceived husband. At the same time a new equilibrium is introduced, since adultery acquires the status of a norm.

Keeping to the same level of generality we may observe a similar design in James's stories. Thus in *In the Cage* the stable situation of the telegraphist at the beginning is disturbed by the appearance of Captain Everard, and this disequilibrium reaches its climax during the meeting in the park. At the end of the story equilibrium is re-established by the marriage of Everard and Lady Bradeen: the telegraphist abandons her dreams, leaves her job, and gets married herself shortly afterwards. The initial equilibrium is not identical to the final one: the first permits the telegraphist's dreams and hopes; the second does not.

But in making this summary of the plot of *In the Cage* we have only followed one of the lines of force of the narrative. The other involves the theme of apprenticeship; in contrast to the first, with its ebb-and-flow pattern, this one marks a gradation. At the beginning the telegraphist does not know anything about Captain Everard; at the end she reaches the peak of her knowledge about him. The first movement is a horizontal one, and is composed of the events which fill the telegraphist's life. The second suggests, rather, the image of a vertical spiral; it consists of successive glimpses (not, however, ordered in time) of the life and personality of Captain Everard. In the first the reader's interest is directed towards the future: what will come of the relationship between Everard and the girl? In the second it is turned towards the past: who is Everard, and what has happened to him?

The movement of the tale is the sum of these two lines of force; some events relate to the first, others to the second, and others still relate to both. Thus the girl's conversations with Mrs. Jordan do not advance the 'horizontal' line at all, whilst her meetings with her future husband, Mr. Mudge, relate to this one alone. Evidently the search for knowledge takes precedence over the development of events, so that the 'vertical' tendency is stronger than the 'horizontal'. Now this movement towards the comprehension of events, which replaces the movement of the events themselves, takes us back to the figure in the carpet: the presence of a quest, and the absence of its object. The 'essence' of the events is not given to us straightaway; each fact, each phenomenon first appears surrounded by an aura of mystery; our interest, naturally, is directed towards 'being', not towards 'doing'.

We now come finally to James's 'style', which has always been described as excessively complex, obscure, unnecessarily difficult. In fact at this level too James surrounds the 'truth', the event itself (which is frequently summed up in the main clause), with a number of subordinate clauses, each of which is simple in itself, but which produce, in their accumulation, an effect of complexity. However, these subordinate clauses are necessary because they illustrate the many intermediary stages which must be passed before one reaches the 'kernel'. Here is an example from the same story:

> There were times when all the wires in the country seemed to start from the little hole-and-corner where she plied for a livelihood, and where, in the shuffle of feet, the flutter of 'forms', the straying of stamps and the ring of change over the counter, the people she had fallen into the habit of remembering and fitting together with others, and of having her theories and interpretations of, kept up before her their long procession and rotation (p. 153).

If we extract the principal proposition of this entangled sentence, we have: 'There were times when . . . the people . . . kept up before her their long procession and rotation.' But around this flat, banal 'truth' James accumulates innumerable details and observations which are much more present than the principal proposition itself, the 'kernel' which as an absolute cause has occasioned this movement, but which none the less remains a quasi-absence. An American stylistician, R. Ohmann, has suggested that much of the complexity of James's style is due to this tendency to 'self-embedding', the 'embedded' elements having a much greater importance than the main part of the sentence.[15] We may go further and say that the complexity of James's style depends entirely on this constructive principle, and not at all on any referential, for instance psychological, complexity. The 'style' and the 'sentiments', the 'form' and the 'content' all say the same thing. They all repeat the same figure in the carpet.

This variant of our general theme allows us to penetrate the secret: at the end of the story Peter Baron acquires the information, the search for which constituted its mainspring; equally, if absolutely necessary, the telegraphist could have found out the truth about Captain Everard. We are, then, in the domain of the *hidden*; but there are other instances in which the 'absence' cannot be overcome by human means, instances where the absolute cause is a *ghost*. There is no risk of such a hero passing as it were unnoticed; the whole text organizes itself around the search for him.

We could go further and say that, if this ever-absent cause is to become present, it *has* to be a ghost. For, curiously enough, Henry James always speaks of ghosts as *presences*. Here are some sentences taken at random from various stories dealing with ghosts: 'I felt his presence as a strong appeal, almost an oppression.'[16] 'A perfect presence... A splendid presence.'[17] 'The hideous plain presence...'[18] 'He was absolutely, on this occasion, a living, detestable, dangerous presence.'[19] '... The spot where he had turned cold with the extinction of his last pulse of doubt as to there being in the place another presence than his own.'[20] 'The image of the "presence", whatever it was, waiting there for him to go—this image had not yet been so concrete for his nerves as when he stopped short of the point at which certainty would have come to him.'[21] 'Wasn't he now in the *most* immediate presence of some inconceivable occult activity?'[22] 'It gloomed, it loomed, it was something, it was somebody, the prodigy of a personal presence.'[23] And finally, this lapidary and falsely tautological formula: 'The presence before him was a presence.'[24] The essence is never present except when it is a ghost, that is, when it is absence *par excellence*.

Any one of James's ghost stories can prove to us the intensity of this presence. *Sir Edmund Orme* (1891)[25] tells the story of a young man who suddenly sees, at the side of Charlotte Marden, the girl that he loves, a strange pale man who, curiously, passes unobserved by everyone except him. The first time this half-visible, half-invisible character sits down next to Charlotte in a church ('He was a pale young man in black, with the air of a gentleman' (p. 128)). He appears again a little later in a reception-room:

> He held himself with a kind of habitual majesty, as if he were different from us... He stood there without speaking—young, pale, handsome, clean-shaven, decorous, with extraordinary light blue eyes and something old-fashioned, like a portrait of years ago, in his head, his manner of wearing his hair. He was in complete mourning... and he carried his hat in his hand (pp. 133–4).

He joins the most intimate conversations between the young couple: 'He stood there... looking at me with the expressionless attention which borrowed its sternness from his sombre distinction' (p. 139). The narrator concludes: 'Of what transcendent essence he was composed I knew not; I have no theory about him (leaving that to others), any more than I have one about such or such another of my fellow-mortals whom I have elbowed in life. He was as positive, as individual, as ultimate a fact as any of these' (p. 145).

This 'presence' of the ghost, one can guess, determines the evolution of the relationship between the narrator and Charlotte and, more generally, the development of the story as a whole. Charlotte's mother also sees the ghost, and recognizes it; it is the ghost of a young man who loved her, who committed suicide because she rejected him. The ghost returns to make sure that such feminine coquetry will not play the same trick on the suitor of the daughter of the woman who caused his death. In the end Charlotte decides to marry the narrator, the mother dies, and the ghost of Sir Edmund Orme disappears.

The tale of the fantastic is a form which lends itself well to James's design. Unlike tales of the marvellous (such as those of the *Thousand and One Nights*), it is characterized not by the mere presence of supernatural beings or phenomena, but by the hesitation that governs the reader's perception of the events represented in it. Throughout the story the reader asks himself (and often, within the book, a character does too) whether the facts which are recounted are to be attributed to natural or to supernatural causes, whether it is a matter of illusion or reality. This hesitation derives from the fact that the extraordinary (and thus potentially supernatural) event occurs not in a marvellous world, but in a familiar, everyday context. The tale of the fantastic is therefore the story of a perception, and we have already seen how such a construction can be directly fitted into James's 'figure in the carpet'.

A tale like *Sir Edmund Orme* conforms fairly closely to this general description of the fantastic genre. A good many of the occult presence's appearances cause the narrator to hesitate, and his hesitation is crystallized in sentences of the 'either . . . or' type: 'It was either all a mistake or Sir Edmund Orme had vanished' (p. 148). Or: 'Was the sound I heard when Chartie shrieked—the other and still more tragic sound I mean—the despairing cry of the poor lady's death-shock or the articulate sob (it was like a waft from a great tempest), of the exorcised and pacified spirit?' (p. 151). And so on.

Henry James's text has other characteristics in common with the genre of the fantastic in general. There is, for instance, a tendency to allegory (which, however, never becomes very strong or it would destroy the fantastic element), so that one sometimes wonders whether his is not simply a morality tale. The narrator interprets the whole episode thus: 'It was a case of retributive justice. The mother was to pay, in suffering, for the suffering she had inflicted, and as the disposition to jilt a lover might have been transmitted to the daughter, the daughter was to be watched, so that *she* might be made to suffer should she do an equal wrong' (p. 146).

Similarly the story follows the gradation of supernatural appearances common to the tale of the fantastic; the narrator is present within the work itself, thus making it easier to integrate the reader into the world of the story; the allusions to the supernatural scattered throughout the text prepare us for an acceptance of it. But apart from these features which link James's tale with the fantastic genre, there are others which distinguish it from it, and which help to define its specific character. We can see this best in another text, the longest of the tales and probably the most famous: *The Turn of the Screw* (1896).[26]

The ambiguity of this story is just as important as that of *Sir Edmund Orme*. The narrator is a young woman, the governess of two children on a country estate. At a certain moment she realizes that the house in which they live is haunted by two former servants, now dead, of depraved morals. These two apparitions are all the more formidable for having established some sort of contact with the children, though the children pretend not to know about it. The governess has no doubts whatever concerning their presence ('It was not, I am sure today as I was sure then, my mere infernal imagination . . .' (pp. 84–5). Or again: 'Even while she spoke the hideous plain presence stood undimmed and undaunted' (p. 115)). To support her conviction she finds perfectly rational arguments:

> Late that night, while the house slept, we had another talk in my room; when she went all the way with me as to its being beyond doubt that I had seen exactly what I had seen. To hold her perfectly in the pinch of that, I found, I had only to ask her how, if I had 'made it up', I came to be able to give, of each of the persons appearing to me, a picture disclosing, to the last detail, their special marks—a portrait on the exhibition of which she had instantly recognized and named them (p. 61).

The governess tries to exorcise the children: as a result one falls seriously ill, whilst only death can 'purify' the other.

However, this same series of events could be presented in an entirely different manner, avoiding altogether the introduction of infernal forces into the story. For the governess's testimony is continually contradicted by that of the other characters ('What a dreadful turn, to be sure, Miss! Where on earth do you see anything?', the housekeeper exclaims (p. 115); and on the same occasion one of the children, Flora, cries: 'I don't know what you mean. I see nobody. I see nothing. I never *have*' (p. 116)). This contradiction reaches such a point that at the end the governess herself has a terrifying suspicion: 'Within a minute there had come to me out of my very pity the appalling alarm of his being perhaps innocent. It was for the instant confounding and bottomless, for if he *were* innocent, what then on earth was *I*?' (p. 136).

It is not of course difficult to find realistic explanations for the governess's hallucinations. She is an excitable and hypersensitive person, and, on the other hand, dreaming up this danger is the only way of bringing the children's uncle, with whom she is secretly in love, to the estate. She herself feels the need to defend herself against a possible accusation of insanity: 'She accepted without directly impugning my sanity the truth as I gave it to her', she says of the housekeeper (p. 48); and later: 'I go on, I know, as if I were crazy; and it's a wonder I'm not' (p. 81). If we add to this the fact that the apparitions always occur at twilight or even during the night and that, on the other hand, certain of the children's reactions which might otherwise seem strange could easily be explained by the governess's own power of suggestion, the story would retain nothing of the supernatural, and we should simply be faced with the account of a neurosis.

This possibility of a double interpretation of the tale has given rise to interminable discussions among its critics: do the ghosts really exist in *The Turn of the Screw*, or do they not? Yet the answer is obvious: in preserving this ambiguity at the very heart of the story James has simply followed the rules of the genre. Not everything in this story, however, is conventional. Whereas the classic nineteenth-century tale of the fantastic has as its principal and explicit theme the hesitation of the protagonist, in James's work the representation of such hesitation is virtually eliminated, and only survives in the reader. The narrators of *Sir Edmund Orme* and of *The Turn of the Screw* are both convinced of the reality of their visions.

At the same time we find in this text those same features of James's narrative as we have already observed elsewhere. Not only is the whole story based on the two ghostly characters, Miss Jessel and Peter Quint, but, for the governess, the essential question is whether the children have perceived the ghosts as well. In the quest which forms the subject of the story perception and knowledge take the place of the object which is, or is to be, perceived. The governess is less terrified by the vision of Peter Quint than by the possibility that the children should also have seen him. Similarly in *Sir Edmund*

*Orme* the mother of Charlotte Marden is less afraid of the sight of the ghost than she is that it should appear to her daughter.

The source of evil (and also of the action) in the story remains hidden: it is the vices of the two dead employees, unnamed vices which are transmitted to the children ('strange passages and perils, secret disorders, vices more than suspected' (pp. 52–3)). The acuteness of the danger is due precisely to the absence of any information about it: 'What it was most impossible to get rid of was the cruel idea that, whatever I had seen, Miles and Flora saw *more*—things terrible and unguessable and that sprang from dreadful passages of intercourse in the past' (pp. 88–9).

To the question as to what really happened at Bly James answers in an oblique fashion: he casts doubt on the word *really*, and affirms the uncertainty of the experience in contrast to the stability—but also the absence—of the essence. One does not even have the right to say that the governess is such-and-such, or that Peter Quint is not. In this world the verb *to be* has lost one of its functions, that of affirming the existence or non-existence of an object. None of our truths is better founded than that of the governess; it may be that the phantom existed, but little Miles paid with his life for the attempt to eliminate the uncertainty as to whether it did or not.[27]

The first variant of our figure in the carpet involved a natural and relative absence: the nature of the secret was such that it was not inconceivable that it should be penetrated. The second variant, on the other hand, described the absolute and supernatural absence of a ghost. A third variant presents us with an absence which is both absolute and natural: *death*.

We can observe this first of all in a tale which is very close to the 'fantastic' variant: *The Friends of the Friends*[28] (1896). A man has seen the ghost of his mother at the moment of her death, and a woman has had the same experience with her father. Struck by this coincidence their common friends—the narrator in particular—try to organize a meeting between them. But all efforts fail to bring them together, each time, as it happens, for the most harmless of reasons. The woman dies, and the man (who is also engaged to the female narrator) claims to have met her on the day of her death. Was it a living being or a ghost that he met? No one will ever know the answer, and as a result of this meeting the engagement between the man and the narrator is broken off.

While both of them were alive, a meeting between them—their love—was impossible. Physical presence would have destroyed life. Not that they knew this in advance: they tried, though always in vain, to meet, but after a final effort, which fails because of the narrator's fear, the woman resigns herself to her fate: 'I shall never, never see him' (p. 383). A few hours later she is dead, as if death were a necessary condition for their meeting to take place (just as they both met their parents as these were about to die). The moment that life (an insignificant presence) ends, there comes the triumph of that essential absence, death. If one believes the man, the woman visited him between ten and eleven in the evening, without saying a word; at midnight she was dead. The narrator has to decide whether this meeting 'really' took place, or whether it is of the same nature as the meetings with the dying parents. She would like to opt for the first solution ('It is remarkable that for a moment, though only for a moment, I found relief in the more personal, as it were, but also the more natural of the two odd facts' (p. 388)); however, this relief does not last, for she realizes that this version of events is too easy, and fails to explain the change which has taken place in her friend.

One cannot speak of death *in itself*; one always dies for someone. 'She's buried, but she's not dead. She's dead for the world—she's dead for me. But she's not dead for *you*', says the narrator (p. 397). And: 'My unextinguished jealousy—that was the Medusa-mask. It hadn't died with her death, it had lividly survived, and it was fed by suspicions unspeakable' (p. 397). And she is right, for this meeting which had never taken place in life gives birth to an incredible love. All that we know about it is what the narrator herself believes, but she succeeds in convincing us: 'How *can* you hide it when you're abjectly in love with her, when you're sick almost to death with the joy of what she gives you? . . . You love her as you've *never* loved, and, passion for passion, she gives it straight back!' (p. 400). Her fiancé does not dare deny this, and the engagement is broken off. The next stage is rapidly reached: since only death can provide the conditions for the man's love, he takes refuge in it himself.

When six years later, in solitude and silence, I heard of his death I hailed it as a direct contribution to my theory. It was sudden, it was never properly accounted for, it was surrounded by circumstances in which—for oh, I took them to pieces!—I distinctly read an intenion, the mark of his own hidden hand. It was the result of a long necessity, of an unquenchable desire. To say exactly what I mean, it was a response to an irresistible call (pp. 400–1).

Death makes a character become the absolute and absent cause of life. More still, death is the source of life, and love is born out of death instead of being interrupted by it. This romantic theme (that of Gautier's *Spirite*) reaches its fullest development in *Maud-Evelyn* (1900).[29] This tale tells the story of a young man, Marmaduke, who falls in love with Maud-Evelyn, a young girl who died fifteen years before he even learned of her existence. (One might note how often the title of a tale puts into relief the absent, essential character in it: *Sir Dominick Ferrand, Sir Edmund Orme, Maud-Eveyln*; and similarly in other stories, like *Nona Vincent*.)

Marmaduke's love, and therefore the 'reality' of Maud-Evelyn, goes through all the stages of a gradation. At the beginning Marmaduke merely admires the girl's parents, who behave as if she were not dead at all; then he begins to think as they do; finally, to use the words of his former friend Lavinia: 'He thinks he knew her' (p. 61). A little later Lavinia declares: 'He *was* in love with her' (p. 62). Next comes their 'marriage', after which Maud-Evelyn 'dies' ('He has lost his wife', Lavinia says (p. 70), in order to explain the fact that he is in mourning). Marmaduke dies in his turn, but Lavinia takes his belief over herself.

In James's usual manner the absent central character of the story, Maud-Evelyn, is viewed not directly, but through a series of multiple reflections. The story is told by a certain Lady Emma, who derives her impressions from her conversations with Lavinia, who in turn meets Marmaduke. He, moreover, only knows Maud-Evelyn's parents, the Dedricks, who evoke the memory of their dead daughter. Thus the 'truth' is four times deformed. Besides, these 'visions' are not identical, but constitute a gradation in themselves. For Lady Emma Marmaduke's behaviour is mere folly ('Was he altogether silly or was he only altogether mercenary?' (p. 57)). She lives in a world in which the imaginary and the real form two distinct and separate blocks. Lavinia adheres to the same standards, but she is prepared to accept Marmaduke's act because she judges it to be beautiful: 'It's self-deception, no doubt, but it comes from something that . . . is beautiful when one does hear of it' (p. 63). And later she says: 'Of course it's only an idea, . . . but it seems to me a beautiful one' (p. 71). For Marmaduke himself death is not a step into non-being; on the contrary, death allowed him to have the most extraordinary of experiences ('The moral appeared to be that nothing in the way of human experience of the exquisite could again particularly matter' (p. 65)). Finally the Dedricks take Maud-Evelyn's existence quite literally, communicating with her through mediums, etc. James has illustrated here, therefore, four possible attitudes towards the imaginary or, alternatively, towards the figurative sense of an expression: the realistic attitude of refusal and condemnation, the aestheticizing attitude of admiration mingled with incredulity, the poetic attitude which admits the coexistence of being and non-being, and finally the naïve attitude which interprets the figurative meaning literally.

We have seen that, in their composition, James's stories are turned towards the past: the quest for an essential and permanently evanescent secret implies that the tale should be an exploration of the past rather than a progression into the future. In *Maud-Evelyn* the past becomes a thematic element, and its glorification one of the principal subjects of the story. Maud-Evelyn's second life is the result of this exploration: 'It's the gradual effect of brooding over the past; the past, that way, grows and grows' (p. 62). There are no limits to the enrichment which the past offers, which is why the parents of Maud-Evelyn act as they do. Marmaduke says: 'You see, they couldn't do much, the old people—and they can do still less now—with the future; so they had to do what they could with the past' (p. 67). And he concludes: 'The more we live in the past, the more things we find in it' (p. 70). To 'limit' oneself to the past is to deny the originality of events, to consider that one lives in a world of memories. Following the chain of reactions to discover the initial motive, the absolute beginning, one comes up suddenly against death, the end *par excellence*. Death is the origin and essence of life, the past is the future of the present, the answer precedes the question.

James wrote another story, a veritable requiem which undoubtedly merits first place among his explorations of the life of the dead: *The Altar of the Dead* (1896).[30] Nowhere else is the force of death, the presence of absence, so intensely affirmed. Stransom, the principal character of this tale, lives in the cult of the dead. All he knows is absence and he prefers it to everything else. His fiancée died before the first 'bridal embrace' (p. 231); but Stransom's life has not suffered as a result, and he enjoys being 'for ever widowed' (ibid.). His life was still 'ruled by a pale ghost, it was still ordered by a sovereign presence' (ibid.); it is organized perfectly around its 'central hollow' (p. 249).

One day he meets a friend, Paul Creston, widowed a few months beforehand. Suddenly he notices beside him another woman whom his friend introduces with some embarrassment as his new wife. This replacement of a sublime absence by a vulgar presence shocks Stransom deeply. 'That new woman, that hired performer, Mrs. Creston? Mrs. Creston had been more living for him than any woman but one . . . He felt quite determined, as he walked away, never in his life to go near her. She was perhaps a human being, but Creston oughtn't to have shown her without precautions, oughtn't indeed to have shown her at all' (p. 235). For him the new wife, the presence, is a forgery, a 'wife for foreign service or purely external use' (p. 236); it is monstrous to have substituted her for the memory of the absent woman.

Little by little Stransom enlarges and elaborates his cult of the dead. He wants to perform 'some material act' (p. 239), and decides to dedicate an altar to them. Each of his many dead friends ('He had perhaps not had more losses than most men, but he had counted his losses more' (p. 232)) is given a candle, and Stransom sinks into an attitude of admiring contemplation in front of them. Stransom's pleasure is even greater than he had expected, because he can thus reintegrate his past:

> Half the satisfaction of the spot for this mysterious and fitful worshipper was that he found the years of his life there, and the ties, the affections, the struggles, the submissions, the conquests, if there had been such, a record of that adventurous journey in which the beginnings and the endings of human relations are the lettered milestones (pp. 241–2).

Another reason is that death is a purification ('The fellow had only had to die for everything that was ugly in him to be washed out in a torrent' (p. 260)), and that death renders possible, finally, the establishment of the harmony which is the end of life. The dead represented by the candles are infinitely close to him: 'Various persons in whom his interest had not been intense drew closer to him by entering this company.' And as a natural consequence 'he almost caught himself wishing that certain of his friends would now die, that he might establish with them in this manner a connection more charming than, as it happened, it was possible to enjoy with them in life' (p. 242).

Only one further step remains to be taken, and Stransom is not held up by it: that of envisaging his own death. He has already begun to dream of this 'rich future' (p. 265): '"The chapel will never be full till a candle is set up before which all the others will pale. It will be the tallest candle of all." Her mild wonder rested on him. "What candle do you mean?" "I mean, dear lady, my own"' (p. 250).

Suddenly a false note enters into this praise of death. Stransom meets, in front of his altar, a lady in mourning who attracts him precisely on account of her devotion to the dead. But when this acquaintance becomes more intimate, he learns that the lady mourns for one person alone, Acton Hague, a formerly intimate friend of Stransom's with whom he had violently quarrelled, and the only dead friend for whom he has never lit a candle. The woman realizes this as well, and the charm of their relationship is broken. Death is present: 'Acton Hague was between them, that was the essence of the matter; and he was never so much between them as when they were face to face' (p. 263). Thus the woman is forced to choose between Stransom and Hague (she prefers Hague), and Stransom to choose between the resentment he feels towards Hague and his affection for the woman (his resentment gets the upper hand). And so we have this moving dialogue: '"Will you give him his candle?" she asked . . . "I can't do that!" he declared at last. "Then good-bye"' (p. 258). It is death that determines the life of the living. At the same time the living do not cease to act upon the life of the dead (since interpenetration is possible in both directions). As soon as his friend abandons him, Stransom discovers that his affection for the dead disappears: 'All the lights had gone out—all his Dead had died again' (p. 266).

One further step, therefore, remains to be taken. After falling seriously ill, Stransom returns to the church, having made up his mind to forgive Acton Hague. He finds his friend there, and a corresponding change has occurred in her as well: she is prepared to forget her one Dead, and to devote herself to the cult of *the* dead. Thus this cult reaches its ultimate sublimation: love, friendship, or resentment no longer govern it; death is glorified in its pure state, without any regard for those whom it has touched. Forgiveness has removed the final barrier on the road to death.

So Stransom can entrust his own life to his friend and die; he expires in her arms, whilst she feels a great dread seize hold of her heart.

We now come to the final variant of our 'figure in the carpet': that in which the place occupied successively by the hidden, the ghost, and by death, is taken by the *work of art*. And if the short story tends in general, more than the novel, to become a theoretical statement, James's tales about art are veritable aesthetic treatises.

*The Real Thing* (1892)[31] is a fairly simple parable. The narrator, a painter, receives a visit one day from a couple who bear every sign of nobility. They ask if they might pose for any book-illustrations that he might be doing, since they are reduced to a state of extreme poverty. They are sure of fitting this role well, for the painter has to depict figures belonging precisely to the leisured classes to which they themselves previously belonged. 'We thought', the husband says, 'that if you ever have to do people like us, we might be something like it. *She*, particularly—for a lady in a book, you know' (p. 233).

The couple are indeed the 'real thing', but this does not in any way facilitate the painter's task. On the contrary, his illustrations become worse and worse, until one day one of his friends points out to him that the fault is perhaps his models'. On the other hand his other models have nothing 'real' about them, but they none the less inspire the most successful illustrations. One Miss Churm was 'only a freckled cockney, but she could represent everything, from a fine lady to a shepherdess' (p. 239). A vagabond Italian named Oronte is also perfectly suited to illustrations of princes and gentlemen.

The absence of 'real' qualities in Miss Churm and Oronte is precisely what gives them their essential value, so necessary to the work of art; whereas the presence of such qualities in the more distinguished models can only be superfluous. The painter explains this by his 'innate preference for the represented subject over the real one: the defect of the real one was so apt to be a lack of representation. I liked things that appeared; then one was sure. Whether they *were* or not was a subordinate and always a profitless question' (p. 237). So it is that, at the end, we find the two uncultivated and low-born characters playing 'noble' parts to perfection, while the 'noble' models do the washing up, following the 'perverse and cruel law in virtue of which the real thing could be so much less precious than the unreal' (p. 258).

Art therefore is not the reproduction of a given 'reality', nor is it created through the imitation of such a reality. It demands quite different qualities; to be 'real' can even, as in the present case, be harmful. In the realm of art there is nothing preliminary to the work, nothing which constitutes its origin. It is the work of art itself that is original; the secondary becomes primary. Hence the frequent comparisons in James's work that explain 'nature' through 'art', for instance:

That was the way many things struck me at that time, in England—as reproductions of something that existed primarily in art or literature. It was not the picture, the poem, the fictive page, that seemed to me a copy; these things were the originals and the life of happy and distinguished people was fashioned in their image.[32]

Several other stories, in particular *The Death of the Lion* (1894),[33] take up the problem of art and life, but from another point of view, that of the relationship between an author's life and his work. A writer becomes famous towards the end of his days; however, the public's interest in him relates not to his work but only to his life. Journalists ask him avidly for details of his personal existence, and his admirers prefer to see the man to reading his books. The ending of the story, at once sublime and grotesque, shows the profound indifference felt for the work by those very persons who, in admiring its author, claim to admire the work as well. This misapprehension has fatal consequences: not only can the writer no longer write after his 'success', but at the end he is killed (literally) by his adorers.

'The artist's life's his work, and this is the place to observe him', says the narrator, a young writer himself (p. 91). Later he makes a similar point: 'Let whoever would represent the interest in his presence . . . I should represent the interest in his work—in other words in his absence' (p. 95). These words merit reflection. Psychological criticism (which, after 'realistic' criticism, is here brought into question) considers the work as a presence—although of little importance in itself—and the author as its absent and absolute cause. James reverses the relationship: the author's life is only an appearance, a contingency, an accident; it is an inessential presence. The work of art is the truth to be sought after, even if there is no hope of finding it. To understand a work better it is no use knowing its author; on the contrary, this course of action kills both the man (Paraday dies) and the work (the manuscript is lost).

The same problem lies at the heart of the story *The Private Life* (1892)[34] where the configuration of absence and presence is drawn in all its details. Of the two opposed characters in it Lord Mellifont is a man of the world; his existence is all presence, all inessential. He is the most agreeable of companions; his conversation is rich, relaxed, and instructive. But it would be vain to try and find anything deep or personal in him; he only exists as a function of others. He has a splendid presence, but it dissimulates nothing, so much so that no one ever succeeds in observing him alone. 'He's there from the moment he knows somebody else is', one of the characters says of him (p. 218); as soon as he is alone he ceases to be.

Beside him Clare Vawdrey exemplifies the other possible combination of presence and absence, a combination which is possible because of the fact that he is a writer and creates works of art. This great writer's presence is mediocre, null; his behaviour does not correspond in any way at all to his work. For instance the narrator tells of being alone with him during a mountain storm:

> Clare Vawdrey was disappointing. I don't know exactly what I should have predicated of a great author exposed to the fury of the elements, I can't say what particular Manfred attitude I should have expected my companion to assume, but it seemed to me somehow that I shouldn't have looked to him to regale me in such a situation with stories (which I had already heard), about the celebrated Lady Ringrose (p. 225).

However, this Clare Vawdrey is not the 'real' one; at the same time as the narrator is exchanging literary gossip with him, another Clare is sitting in front of his desk writing pages of magnificent prose. 'The world was vulgar and stupid, and the real man would have been a fool to come out for it when he could gossip and dine by deputy' (ibid.).

The contrast is thus complete: Clare Vawdrey is double, and Lord Mellifont is not even single. 'He [Lord Mellifont] was all public and had no corresponding private life, just as Clare Vawdrey was all private and had no corresponding public one' (p. 212). We have here, then, the two complementary aspects of a single movement: the presence is hollow (Lord Mellifont), and the absence is full (the work of art). In the paradigm in which we have inscribed it the work of art has a place all of its own; it is more essential than the hidden, more accessible than the ghost, more material than death; it offers the only way of experiencing essence. The other Clare Vawdrey sitting in the darkness is hidden by the work itself; he is the text that writes itself, the absence that is more present than any other.

The perfect symmetry that forms the basis of this story is characteristic of Henry James's conception of the plot of his tales. They abound, generally, with coincidences and symmetries. One thinks, for instance, of Guy Walsingham, a woman with a male pseudonym, and Dora Forbes, a man with a female pseudonym, in *The Death of the Lion*; of the incredible coincidences by means of which the plot is resolved in *The Tone of Time* (where the two women loved the same man) or *The Altar of the Dead* (where the same dead figure determines the behaviour of the two characters); of the resolution of *Sir Dominick Ferrand*, and so on. We know that for James the interest of the tale lies not in its 'horizontal' movement, but in the 'vertical' exploration of a single event, and this is what explains the conventional and entirely predictable side of his stories.

*The Birthplace* (1903)[35] takes up and develops the theme of *The Death of the Lion*, that of the relation between a work of literature and the life of its author. This story tells of the public cult of the nation's greatest poet, dead now for many centuries; and in particular of the experience of a couple, Mr. and Mrs. Gedge, the keepers of the museum in the poet's 'birthplace'. A true interest in the poet should involve reading and admiring his work; on the other hand in dedicating oneself to his cult, one substitutes an insignificant presence for the essential absence. 'None of Them care tuppence about Him. The only thing They care about is this empty shell—or rather, for it isn't empty, the extraneous, preposterous stuffing of it' (p. 421).

After feeling so happy, originally, because of his admiration for the poet, at being appointed keeper of the museum, Morris Gedge comes to notice the contradiction which lies at the root of the situation. His public duties oblige him to affirm the poet's presence in the house, and its objects; but his love for the poet—and for truth—leads him to question this presence ('I'll be hanged if He's *here*!' (p. 436)). To begin with, almost nothing is known about the poet's life; even the most basic facts about it are surrounded with uncertainty. 'Well, I grant you there was somebody,' Gedge says, 'but the details are naught. The links are missing. The evidence—in particular about that room upstairs, in itself our Casa Santa—is *nil*. It was so awfully long ago' (p. 430). We know neither whether he was actually born in this room, nor even whether he was born at all. So Gedge suggests 'modalising' the speech which in their capacity as guides they deliver to the public. 'Couldn't you adopt . . . a slightly more *discreet* method? What we can say is that things have been *said*; that's all *we* have to do with' (p. 429).

Yet even this attempt to replace the reality of *being* by that which is *said*, by the reality of speech, does not go far enough. One should not regret the lack of information concerning the poet's life; one should be glad at it. The essence of the poet is his work, not his house; it is preferable, therefore, that his house should bear no trace of him whatever. As the wife of a visitor remarks: 'It's rather a pity, you know, that He *isn't* here. I mean as Goethe's at Weimar. For Goethe *is* at Weimar.' To which her husband replies: 'Yes my dear; that's

Goethe's bad luck. There he sticks. *This* man isn't anywhere. I defy you to catch him' (p. 436).

One last stage remains to be passed, and Gedge does not hesitate: 'Practically . . . there *is* no author; that is for us to deal with. There are all the immortal people—*in* the work; but there's nobody else' (p. 439). Not only is the author a product of the work; he is also a useless product. The illusion of *being* must be dispelled: 'There *is* no such Person' (ibid.).

The plot of the story takes up this same idea (which up to now we only saw in Gedge's statements). At the beginning the keeper of the museum tried to tell the public the truth, but all this brought him was the threat of dismissal from his post. So Gedge chooses another way; instead of reducing his little speech to the bare minimum which the facts of the matter permit, he amplifies it to the point of absurdity, inventing non-existent but plausible details about the poet's life in his birthplace. 'It was a way like another, at any rate, of reducing the place to the absurd' (p. 453); exaggeration has the same sense as effacement. But the two ways are distinguished by one important property: whilst the first was simply the statement of the truth, the second has for him all the advantages of art. Gedge's speech is admirable; it is a work of art in itself. Nor is his reward late in coming; instead of being dismissed, Gedge finds his salary doubled at the end of the story, because of everything he has done for the poet.

James's very last tales avoid so categorical a formulation of any opinion whatever. They remain indecisive, ambiguous; the bold colours of earlier years are blurred by new nuances. *The Velvet Glove* (1909)[36] takes up the same problem of the relation between 'art' and 'life', but gives a much less clear answer. John Berridge is a successful writer; in a fashionable *salon* he meets two striking characters, the Lord and the Princess, who, like Olympians descended on to the earth, incarnate everything he has always dreamt of. The Princess flirts a little with Berridge, and he is on the point of losing his head over her when he realizes that she wants only one thing of him, that he should write the preface of her latest novel.

At first sight this tale is a praise of 'life' in contrast to writing. From the very beginning of the reception Berridge says to himself: 'What was the pale page of fiction compared with the intimately personal adventure that, in almost any direction, he [the young Lord] would have been all so stupidly, all so gallantly, all so instinctively . . . ready for?' (p. 237). As for the Princess, he is struck by the

> really 'decadent' perversity, recalling that of the most irresponsibly insolent of the old Romans and Byzantines, that could lead a creature so formed for living and breathing her Romance, and so committed, up to the eyes, to the constant fact of her personal immersion in it and genius for it, the dreadful amateurish dance of ungrammatically scribbling it, with editions and advertisements and reviews and royalties and every other futile item . . . ? (p. 252).

Imagining himself an Olympian as well, Berridge throws as far as possible from him everything to do with writing:

> He would leave his own stuff snugly unread, to begin with; that would be a beautiful start for an Olympian career. He should have been as unable to write those works in short as to make anything else of them; and he should have had no more arithmetic for computing fingers than any perfect-headed marble Apollo mutilated at the wrists. He should have consented to know but the grand personal adventure on the grand personal basis: nothing short of this . . . would begin to be, on any side, Olympian enough (p. 245).

But the moral that Berridge draws is not necessarily the moral of the tale. For one thing, the attitude of this famous writer might usefully be placed side by side with that of the Princess: both of them want to become what they are not. Berridge writes good novels, but sees himself, in his imagination, as a 'prepossessing young shepherd' (p. 247); the Princess lives the life of the Gods, and at the same time wants to be a successful novelist. As James puts it:

> The mysterious values of other types kept looming larger before you than the doubtless often higher but comparatively familiar ones of your own, and if you had anything of the artist's real feeling for life the attraction and the amusement of possibilities so projected were worth more to you, in nineteen moods out of twenty, than the sufficiency, the serenity, the felicity, whatever it might be, of your stale personal certitudes (p. 236).

On the other hand, to describe the 'life' which is thus affirmed in opposition to writing, Berridge (and James) have only one word: 'romantic'. The young Lord's rendezvous must be 'of a high "romantic" order' (p. 237), and he himself resembles 'far-off romantic and "plastic" figures' (p. 248); the adventures of the Princess would have to have the 'absolute attraction of romance'

(p. 245). Thinking that the Princess loves him, it is only in books that Berridge can find an image of his feeling: 'It was ground he had ventured on, scenically, representationally, in the artistic sphere, but without ever dreaming he should "realize" it thus in the social' (p. 253). It is not 'life' that is affirmed in opposition to the novel, but rather the role of a character in relation to that of an author.

Besides John Berridge has as little success in becoming a 'prepossessing shepherd' as the Princess in becoming a popular novelist. Just as Clare Vawdrey, in *The Private Life*, could not be both a great writer and a brilliant man of the world at the same time, so here Berridge must return to the unromantic condition of a novelist, after a romantic gesture (he kisses the Princess), the purpose of which is precisely to prevent her from playing the part of a novelist. Art and life are incompatible; with serene bitterness Berridge exclaims at the end: 'You *are* Romance . . ., so what more do you want?' (p. 263). James leaves it to the reader to decide for himself which of the two alternatives he prefers; and we begin to perceive a possible reversal of the 'figure in the carpet'.

The motive force of Henry James's stories, that which determines their structure, is the essential secret. Moreover this organizing principle becomes itself the explicit theme of at least two of them. These are, as it were, metaliterary stories, stories devoted to the constructive principle of the story.

The first of these—*The Figure in the Carpet*—was discussed at the beginning of this study. The secret whose existence Vereker revealed becomes a motive force in the narrator's life; then in those of his friend, George Corvick, and of his friend's fiancée and wife, Gwendolen Erme; and finally in that of Gwendolen's second husband, Drayton Deane. At one point Corvick claims to have discovered the secret, but dies shortly afterwards. Gwendolen learns the solution shortly before her husband's death, but does not tell it to anyone else, keeping it silent until her own death. Thus at the story's end we are as ignorant as we were at the beginning.

This lack of change is, however, only apparent, for between the beginning and the end there is the tale, that is, the search for the secret. And now we know that Henry James's secret (and, no doubt, Vereker's as well) consists precisely in the existence of a secret as such, of an absolute and absent cause, and in the effort to discover this secret, to make the absence present. Vereker's secret was thus revealed to us, but in the only way possible: if it had been named, it would no longer have existed, and it is precisely its existence that constitutes the secret. The secret is by definition inviolable, because it consists in the very fact that it exists. The quest of the secret must never finish, because it is identical with the secret itself. Some critics have already interpreted *The Figure in the Carpet* in this sense; thus Blackmur spoke of the 'exasperation of the mystery without the presence of mystery';[37] Blanchot refers to this 'art which cannot be deciphered, but is itself the cipher of the indecipherable';[38] and, with a greater degree of precision, Philippe Sollers explains it thus: 'The solution of the problem which is expounded to us is nothing other than the exposition of the problem itself.'[39]

On a more serious note, the same answer is taken up once again, and this time with a greater degree of nuance, in *The Beast in the Jungle* (1903).[40] John Marcher believes that some unknown but essential event is going to occur in his life, and he organizes it entirely around this future moment. His friend May Bartram describes his feeling thus: 'You said you had had from your earliest time, as the deepest thing within you, the sense of being kept for something rare and strange, possibly prodigious and terrible, that was sooner or later to happen to you, that you had in your bones the foreboding and the conviction of, and that would perhaps overwhelm you' (p. 359).

May Bartram decides to join with Marcher in his watching for this event. He is very appreciative of her solicitude, and does not fail to wonder sometimes if this strange thing is connected with her. Thus when she moves into a house nearer to him, it occurs to him that 'perhaps the great thing he had so long felt as in the lap of the gods was no more than this circumstance, which touched him so nearly, of her acquiring a house in London' (p. 366). Similarly, when she falls ill, he 'caught himself—for he *had* so done—*really* wondering if the great accident would take form now as nothing more than his being condemned to see this charming woman, this admirable friend, pass away from him' (p. 378). As her death approaches, this fear becomes almost a conviction: 'Her dying, her death, his consequent solitude—*that* was what he had figured as the beast in the jungle, that was what had been in the lap of the gods' (p. 388).

However, this supposition never becomes a complete certainty, and Marcher, whilst appreciating May Bartram's efforts to help him, still continues to pass his life in an endless state of waiting. Before dying

May tells him that the Thing is no longer there to be waited for, but that it has already happened. Marcher has the same feeling, but tries in vain to understand what this Thing consists in. Finally one day in front of May's tomb the revelation comes: 'All the while he had waited the wait was itself his portion' (p. 401). The secret is the existence of the secret itself. Horrified by this realization, Marcher throws himself sobbing on to the tomb, and the story finishes with this picture.

'It wouldn't have been failure to be bankrupt, dishonoured, pilloried, hanged; it was failure not to be anything' (p. 379). Marcher could have avoided this; it would have been enough to pay a different sort of attention to May's existence. She was not the hidden secret, as he had sometimes thought; but by loving her he would have been able to avoid the mortal despair with which he was seized at the sight of the truth. May had understood this: in loving him she had found the secret of her life; helping Marcher in his search was her 'essential thing'. She asked for nothing better than to be interested in him, and in the end she has her reward: 'I'm more sure than ever my curiosity, as you call it, will be but too well repaid' (p. 371). Marcher does not know how right he is when he says, dismayed at the idea of her death, that her absence would be 'the absence of everything' (p. 391). The search for the secret and for truth is never anything but a search, a search without any content whatever; May Bartram's life, on the other hand, has as its content her love for Marcher. The figure which we have observed in the course of our examination of the stories reaches here its ultimate, supreme form, which is at the same time its dialectical negation.

If Henry James's secret, the figure in the carpet of his work, the string on which the pearls of the individual stories are strung, if this secret is precisely the existence of a secret, how is it that we can now name it, and make the absence present? Are we not thus betraying James's fundamental precept, which consists in this affirmation of the absence, of the impossibility of describing the truth by its name? But criticism too (including ours) has always obeyed the same law. It is the search for truth, not its revelation—the quest for the treasure rather than the treasure itself, for the treasure can only be absent. Thus, once we have finished this 'reading' of James, we must begin to read him, and throw ourselves into the quest for the sense of his work, though knowing as we do that this sense is nothing other than the quest itself.

NOTES

1. For instance, Gérard Genette's essays in his *Figures*, i, ii, and iii (Seuil, Paris, 1966, 1969, 1972); my contribution to the volume *Qu'est-ce que le structuralisme?* (Seuil, Paris, 1968), and some of the studies collected together in my *Poétique de la prose* (Seuil, Paris, 1971).
2. The following pages are a somewhat abridged version of the study 'Le Secret du récit' in *Poétique de la prose*, pp. 151–85 (Ed.).
3. *The Complete Tales of Henry James*, ed. Leon Edel (Rupert Hart-Davis, London, 1962–4), ix. 273–315. Except where a contrary indication is given, all references in the following pages to James's tales will be to this edition (to be given as *Tales*) (Ed.).
4. *Tales*, viii. 343–405.
5. *Tales*, x. 139–242.
6. I have here used the words 'point of view', 'perception', and 'vision' (the last used by James himself) to translate the single French word *vision* (Ed.).
7. Letter to Mrs. Humphry Ward (July 1899), quoted from Edith Wharton, 'The Man of Letters', in *Henry James, A Collection of Critical Essays*, ed. Leon Edel (Prentice-Hall, Englewood Cliffs, N.J., 1963), p. 34.
8. *The Novels and Tales of Henry James*, New York edition (Macmillan, London, 1909), vol. xi, pp. xvii–xviii.
9. *Tales*, xi. 295–6.
10. From *Brooksmith*, *Tales*, viii. 23.
11. Tr. Andrew Lang (Heinemann, London, 1924), p. 298.
12. (Garnier, Paris, 1964), p. 88.
13. Flaubert himself wrote in a letter: 'Have you ever believed in the existence of things? Is not everything illusion? There is no truth except in "relations", that is, in the way in which we perceive objects' (to Maupassant, 15 Aug. 1878). Tr. from G. Flaubert, *Correspondance*, viii (Conard, Paris, 1930), 135.
14. Cf. T. Todorov, *Grammaire du Décaméron* (Mouton, The Hague, 1969) (Ed.).
15. R. Ohmann, 'Generative Grammars and the Concept of Literary Style', *Word*, xx (1964), 436–7.
16. From *Sir Edmund Orme*, *Tales*, viii. 133–4.
17. Ibid., p. 135.
18. *The Turn of the Screw*, *Tales*, x. 115.
19. Ibid., p. 71.
20. *The Jolly Corner*, *Tales*, xii. 221.
21. Ibid.
22. Ibid., p. 224.
23. Ibid.
24. Ibid., p. 226.
25. *Tales*, viii. 119–51.
26. *Tales*, x. 15–138.
27. For a fuller treatment of James's ghost stories, see my essay 'Les Fantômes de Henry James' in *Poétique de la prose*, pp. 186–96.

28. Originally entitled *The Way it Came*. In *Tales*, ix. 371–401.
29. *Tales*, xi. 43–75.
30. *Tales*, ix. 231–71.
31. *Tales*, viii. 229–58.
32. From *The Author of 'Beltraffio'*, *Tales*, v. 307.
33. *Tales*, ix. 77–118.
34. *Tales*, viii. 189–227.
35. *Tales*, xi. 403–65.
36. *Tales*, xii. 233–65.
37. R. P. Blackmur, 'In the Country of the Blue', *The Kenyon Review*, v (1943), 609.
38. M. Blanchot, *Le Livre à venir* (Gallimard, Paris, 1959), p. 161.
39. P. Sollers, *Logiques* (Seuil, Paris, 1968), p. 121.
40. *Tales*, xi. 351–402.

# 6 *The Structuralist Sciences and Philosophy*

JOHN MEPHAM

THE dialogue between philosophy and structuralism has probably been at its richest and most productive in relation to the structural anthropology of Lévi-Strauss. Most of what I have to say will be concerned with his work. But I think that an evaluation of it and of its philosophical implications is possible only if it is considered in a very broad perspective. This will involve, for example, considering its claims in the light of general problems in epistemology and the philosophy of science. And it will also involve frequent reference to the profound continuity between structural anthropology and the thought of Marx and Freud, a continuity which Lévi-Strauss himself has often insisted upon. So much that has been written on Lévi-Strauss in England has concentrated more or less exclusively on the significance of his work considered only as a moment in the development of a particular science, anthropology, and fails to capture the sense in which it is an aspect of a broader movement in Western thought and is one manifestation, Freud and Marx being among the others, of a decisive break with traditions of thought that have been dominant in Europe since the seventeenth century.

Structural anthropology claims to be an objective science. To evaluate this claim one would need to have some general account of the logical and epistemological characteristics of scientific theories. In very general terms it might be proposed that a scientific theory should at least satisfy the requirements that it be conceptually rigorous (its terms having precise and unambiguous meanings) and that it be empirically testable. However, it has recently been much disputed whether there are any such general requirements. It is not clear that conceptual rigour might not in fact impede progress in science. Certainly the history of science reveals many cases of important theoretical innovation the very richness and power of which were only possible by virtue of a certain conceptual looseness, that is by the rejection of the strategy of conceptual rigour. Even if such general requirements are accepted it is extremely difficult to give them a clear formulation so that their implications for the evaluation of particular problem cases, such as structuralist theories or psychoanalytic theory, are unambiguous and yet not arbitrary. While there is general agreement that in some sense or other scientific theories are ultimately to be judged by reference to their consistency with empirically discoverable facts, most suggestions as to how this feature of theories should be interpreted have turned out to be unacceptable in one way or another.[1]

It used to be thought that the testability of a scientific theory must consist in the theory's being open to verification or falsification by means of some specifiable set of empirical procedures and by reference to some specifiable set of observable facts. For example it has been claimed that a theory must be formulated in such a way that empirical laws are derivable from it and that predictions of particular matters of empirical fact must serve as the test of whether or not the theory should be accepted. However, both epistemological considerations and the actual history of science have suggested to many philosophers that such formulations of a requirement of testability are unacceptable. This is particularly clear in the case of theories which are both at an early stage of articulation and which are of very broad scope, potentially explanatory of a wide range of different kinds of empirical phenomena (and this is clearly the case with, for example, the theories of structural anthropology and of psychoanalysis). For such theories it is bound to be the case that for a very large range of relevant facts (facts such that the theory definitely claims to be an account of the systems responsible for their production) it is impossible to specify which facts would verify or confirm and which would falsify the theory.

Thus the application of a theory to the explanation of many of the phenomena falling within its range is bound to be speculative, to be an imaginative exercise and not an exercise in deduction and calculation, and thus to be such as to constitute a demonstration of the potential richness and power of the theory and not a parade of acquired and unassailable results. This does not mean, of course, that such demonstrations can ignore very general requirements. They should be logically consistent; they should take note of all available relevant evidence, and so on. It may well be that some of the cases of purported arbitrariness in structuralist or related analyses actually are arbitrary or unacceptable by virtue of ignoring such very general requirements. Therefore it would be important to distinguish between an unfavourable judgement on a particular analysis and a dismissal of structuralism as such, as if such particular cases could show that the basic theories were somehow methodologically flawed. In my own opinion Foucault's *The Order of Things* is in places quite perverse in its failure to take into account what seem to be relevant bits of evidence (the central importance of Newtonian physics in the eighteenth century, for example). Yet these inadequacies, if they are such, do not in themselves show that Foucault's theory concerning the nature of the unity and coherence of thought and discourse is incorrect or unacceptably vague.

Such issues make it very difficult to provide any simple clear-cut defence of the view that structural anthropology and psycho-analysis are in fact objective scientific theories. The problem can be clarified, however, by reference to those features of these theories which derive from the fact that they are theories about systems of representation. We need to look at some of the ways in which explanation and interpretation will have specific features dependent upon the particular properties of such systems. Structural anthropology has in common with psycho-analytic theory 'the conviction that we must work on meanings'.[2] Now it is in general true that the forms of empirical regularity, the study of which can allow the discovery of the underlying coherence of a semantic system, are not correlations or empirical generalizations (as has often been thought to be the case where the systems studied by physics and chemistry are concerned) but are *transformations*. That is to say the view that scientific inquiry must be based on the discovery of empirical general laws is simply quite wrong where the object of investigation happens to be, for example, a linguistic and not a mechanical system. The kinds of relationships which it is for the scientist to investigate, and which impose upon him certain restrictions of method, depend not on a definition of science in general but on the kind of object he happens to be studying. I should say that there can be no such thing as a study of the methodology of science in general. A scientist can only determine what rules should guide his inquiry when he already knows what it is that he is studying. This would mean, for example, that there could be no such thing as an account of the general rules of testability in science, arrived at on the basis of general epistemological or logical considerations, which could be appealed to as proof that historical materialism or psycho-analytic theory are not scientific theories. The sciences of social formations and of the unconscious are no doubt bound to be different from the science of mechanical systems in relation to their account of the conditions under which it is possible to have knowledge of these systems. For example, whether or not it will be possible to discover general laws at the empirical level, to make predictions, to explain individual events or only classes of events, and if so which kinds of classes, whether or not teleological explanation is appropriate, and whether quantification or other forms of mathematical representation are possible: all these things can only be answered not by reference to some preconception of what is to count as scientific knowledge but by an understanding of what, in any particular case, that knowledge is of.[3] After all, the sciences of subatomic systems and of evolutionary biological populations differ in these respects from the science of Newtonian mechanical systems so there is little reason for surprise that other sciences will also.

Thus what may seem like methodological peculiarities of structuralist analysis stem in fact from the particular form of complexity of the systems which underlie and which generate the observed features of social and cultural life requiring explanation. Many of Lévi-Strauss's methodological remarks become quite clear if this is borne in mind. The most general point he makes is that the forms of social life 'consist of systems of behaviour that represent the projection, on the level of conscious and socialized thought, of universal laws which regulate the unconscious activities of the mind'.[4] And these laws are such as to constitute the conditions for the production of various kinds of meaning. It is particularly important to notice the specific kinds of relationships which a theory of such a system postulates between the generative structures on the one hand and the observed 'semantic material' on the other, for it is on the specificity of these relationships that the conditions in which it is possible to understand the observed phenomena, and the methods whereby this can be achieved, depend. For example, the same underlying structures can generate quite different manifest sign systems. This is so for various reasons (e.g. the fact that the elements, the signs, are not determined by the structure, and may be more or less motivated, more or less dependent on inaccessible facts of a historical nature; the fact that it is the *relations* between the elements and not the elements themselves which are significant; the fact that 'messages' are quite likely to be over-determined, and are thus to be analysed in terms of more than one underlying structure, etc.). This is the basis of Lévi-Strauss's 'transformational method'. According to this method when one is considering a group of myths, for example, the problem is not to find inductive generalizations which are true of them or of their elements, but to consider each as a transform of the other, a variant in which change of elements accompanies a preservation of relations, or of relations of relations; and on this basis to ask whether such transformational relations reveal anything about the structures they all have in common at a level which renders them inaccessible to direct empirical observation. That structure is not of the order of observable fact is one of Lévi-Strauss's persistent themes (usually as a criticism of the 'structuralism' of Radcliffe-Brown). As a matter of fact he does not consider this method to be peculiar to the human sciences but discovers it also in the work of Cuvier in palaeontology and comparative anatomy. It may be possible to view it, in fact, as a general description of scientific inquiry which requires particular interpretations in the light of the objects of the particular sciences.

> Aucune science ne peut, aujourd'hui, considérer les structures relevant de son domaine comme se réduisant à un arrangement quelconque de parties quelconques. N'est structuré que l'arrangement répondant à deux conditions: c'est un système, régi par une cohésion interne; et cette cohésion, inaccessible à l'observation d'un système isolé, se révèle dans l'étude des transformations, grâce auxquelles on retrouve des propriétés similaires, dans des systèmes en apparence différents.[5]

Perhaps it is worth emphasizing this point because it is relevant to an understanding of some of the features not only of structural anthropology but also of Marx's theory of social formations and of psycho-analysis—all 'human sciences' in which essential reference is made to systems of representation and their particular properties. Consider, for example, the interpretation of dreams. What is the source of the difficulty we have in evaluating dream interpretations? It stems, in part, from the particular nature of the relationship which psycho-analytic theory postulates between the latent content of a dream and its manifest content, and the nature of the 'dream work' in which this translation comes about. The dream work consists of acting upon latent semantic elements by such processes as condensation and displacement. And the selection of semantic elements which undergo this process is itself the result of the contingencies of a particular person's life-history. There can be, therefore, no question of an interpretation which consists in the identification of latent 'meanings' by a process of decoding the elements of a dream taken in isolation or one at a time. There can be no such thing as a dictionary of dream symbols, in which might be listed all symbols for female pudenda or all father symbols or whatever. Not only can no dream element be decoded taken by itself, no entire dream can be either. In the absence of a series of different dreams and of material given in free association, neurotic symptoms and so on, it would be quite impossible to reconstruct the latent dream content. In fact even with such material available interpretation is in principle interminable (just as, for the same sorts of reasons, is the analysis of myths).[6] But these difficulties in no way show that the theory of the unconscious is not a scientific theory, and no particular set of such difficulties could show that it is not true. The difficulties stem from the form of complexity of the unconscious and its processes and their relation to conscious processes, and not from faulty methodology. From the fact that a theory postulates a relationship between generative structures and manifest phenomena that precludes explanation of individual semantic events, and that precludes unambiguous evaluation even of the interpretation of extended systems of semantic material, it cannot be inferred that such a theory could not be true, but only that if true then the world contains systems of particularly intriguing kinds of complexity. Thus any methodological rule that specified that such a theory should be rejected would be a rule that would reject a possibly true theory and would thus be quite unacceptable. This is, for example, the case with the methodology of Karl Popper.

These problems can be clarified by reference to some general points about fundamental theoretical innovation. In his discussions of the epistemological problems related to structuralist theory Lévi-Strauss has frequently emphasized two points. I think these two points are perfectly general and are not peculiar to the human sciences. I shall refer to them as the demand for specificity and the demand for a theoretical critique of the facts.

Of the demand for specificity Lévi-Strauss has written:[7]

Durkheim fut probablement le premier à introduire, dans les sciences de l'homme, cette exigence de spécificité, qui devait permettre un renouvellement dont la plupart d'entre elles—et singulièrement la linguistique—ont bénéficé au début du xxe siècle. Pour toute forme de pensée et d'activité humaines, on ne peut poser des questions de nature ou d'origine avant d'avoir identifié et analysé les phénomènes, et découvert dans quelle mesure les relations qui les unissent suffisent à les expliquer. Il est impossible de discuter sur un objet, de reconstituer l'histoire qui lui a donné naissance, sans savoir, d'abord, *ce qu'il est*; autrement dit, sans avoir épuisé l'inventaire de ses déterminations internes.

This demand constitutes a principle of methodological antireductivism, although without prejudging the possibilities for eventual relations between sciences at later stages of development. It says that in the first instance a science of a specific domain is based on the discovery of the specific coherence of its object. Before any question of relationships between domains can be discussed meaningfully one must have a theory of the specific difference which marks off one domain from another and which, within a domain, explains the production of the diverse and apparently arbitrary variations.

For example, before any general question about the physiological basis of linguistic behaviour can be discussed we must first have a theory which defines the characteristics of behaviour which are specific to it by virtue of its being linguistic, which specifies the 'internal determinants' of such behaviour, and explains the range and variety characteristic of it. Without such a conception of the hidden unity underlying the empirical diversity we shall be unable even to identify which behaviour is correctly thought of as linguistic, and disputes about such border-line cases will be without scientific interest. Thus it would be impossible to decide whether or not a chimpanzee which has acquired a sizeable vocabulary which it can use to 'converse' with its keepers has or has not 'really' learned a language, or whether or not its putative language is in any way fundamentally different from ours. There will be no way of evaluating observed empirical differences (breadth of vocabulary, use of tenses, etc.). Chomsky's attack on behaviourist theories of verbal behaviour was centred around his claim that the attempt to assimilate the acquisition of a language to other forms of learning or of acquiring skills made it impossible for these theories to account for precisely those central and specific features of language which constitute its specific difference (for example the fact that a speaker of a language has the ability to produce and to recognize a 'virtually' infinite set of novel well-formed sentences in that language).

It was an important feature of much of the speculation in sociology and social anthropology of the later part of the nineteenth century that it ignored the principle that theories of society or culture should be constructed on the basis of the specific differences between human and biological systems. The overwhelming evidence of the physical continuity between *homo sapiens* and other animal species accumulated by the late 1860s seemed to many to support the view that anthropology, the science of man, would be but a sub-branch of zoology. Thus we find, for example, this definition of the science by Tylor:[8]

ANTHROPOLOGY (the *science of man* . . .) denotes the natural history of mankind. In the general classification of knowledge it stands as the highest section of zoology or the science of animals, itself the highest section of biology or the science of living beings . . . Not only are these various sciences [anatomy, physiology, psychology, sociology, etc.] concerned largely with man, but several among them have in fact suffered by the almost entire exclusion of other animals from their scheme. It is undoubted that comparative anatomy and physiology, by treating the human species as one member of a long series of related organisms, have gained a higher and more perfect understanding of man himself and his place in the universe than could have been gained by the narrower investigation of his species by and for itself. It is to be regretted that hitherto certain other sciences—psychology, ethics, and even philology and sociology—have so little followed so profitable an example.

Thus differences between men and animals were taken to be only a matter of degree. Darwin's *The Descent of Man*, for example, is an attempt to show that each of the purported specific characteristics of man, falling under the general heading 'his intellectual and moral faculties', are also exemplified, albeit at a 'low level of development', in animal behaviour. But one cannot understand, for example, the specific coherence of human social relations or behaviour by reference to resemblances they may show at the superficial level to relations or behaviour among animals, any more than one can understand digestion by reference to its superficial resemblance to cooking (in that it consists in a transformation of matter involving heat). Superficial resemblances may conceal fundamental differences of internal structure. Appeal to analogy cannot function as a principle of explanation in the absence of a theory justifying the analogy by reference to similarity of forms of internal coherence. For example, Lévi-Strauss cites this appeal to analogy by Tylor:[9] 'the bow and arrow is a species, the habit of flattening children's skulls is a species, the practice of reckoning numbers by tens is a species. The geographical distribution of these things, and their transmission from region to region, have to be studied as the naturalist studies the geography of his botanical and zoological species.' But Tylor's analogies here have no theoretical legs to stand on. The whole project of Anthropology, conceived of impetuously by Tylor and many others in the late nineteenth century, as the application of the principles of evolutionary biology to the species *homo sapiens*, was thus bound to be a theoretical failure.

Mais rien n'est plus dangereux que cette analogie. Car, même si le développement de la génétique doit permettre de dépasser définitivement la notion d'espèce, ce qui l'a rendue et la rend encore valable pour le naturaliste, c'est que le cheval donne effectivement naissance au cheval, et qu'à travers un nombre suffisant de générations, *Equus caballus* est le descendant réel d'*Hipparion*. La validité historique des reconstructions du naturaliste est garantie, en dernière analyse, par le lien biologique de la reproduction. Au contraire, une hache n'engendre jamais une autre hache; entre deux outils identiques, ou entre deux outils différents mais de forme aussi voisine qu'on voudra, il y a et il y aura toujours une discontinuité radicale, qui provient du fait que l'un n'est pas issu de l'autre, mais chacun d'eux d'un système de représentations.[10]

Unfortunately there is a great deal of modern ethology which is similarly impetuous and dangerous, and which is ideology masquerading as science. Human social relations of production and property systems cannot be understood by an appeal to the phenomena of territoriality among birds. And human kinship systems cannot be understood by an appeal to their basis in purported biological instincts or physiological drives. The problem is not to show that culture is part of nature but to show in exactly what way culture includes but transforms nature, so that what we have in common with other biological organisms enters into our lives only in the form of specifically social and cultural structures.

Parce qu'ils sont des systèmes de symboles, les systèmes de parenté offrent à l'anthropologue un terrain privilégié sur lequel ses efforts peuvent presque (et nous insistons sur ce: presque) rejoindre ceux de la science sociale la plus développée, c'est-à-dire la linguistique. Mais la condition de cette rencontre, dont une meilleure connaissance de l'homme peut être espérée, c'est de ne jamais perdre de vue que, dans le cas de l'étude sociologique comme dans celui de l'étude linguistique nous sommes en plein symbolisme. Or, s'il est légitime, et en un sens inévitable, d'avoir recours à l'interprétation naturaliste pour essayer de comprendre l'émergence de la pensée symbolique, celle-ci une fois donnée, l'explication doit changer aussi radicalement de nature que le phénomène nouvellement apparu diffère de ceux qui l'ont précédé et préparé.[11]

It is only too easy, for example, to see the incest taboo as 'nothing but' the denial of a biological impulse. But not only the denial but also that which it denies can only be understood in terms that transcend individualistic and naturalistic explanation. It is only possible for there to be an incest taboo where individuals are identified and related to in terms of the categories of kinship. Thus it is necessarily located in human life in and through a system of representations which make possible the specific meanings which enter into our conduct and our choices at the conscious level. 'Sans doute, la famille biologique est présente et se prolonge dans la société humaine. Mais ce qui confère à la parenté son caractère de fait social n'est pas ce qu'elle doit conserver de la nature: c'est la démarche essentielle par laquelle elle s'en sépare.'[12]

Specificity is demanded not only at the level of the human as contrasted with the biological sciences, but also *within* the human sciences. This point is important in relation to the problem of the dependence of systems of representation (or 'ideologies' as Lévi-Strauss, following Marx, refers to them) on systems of economic and social organization. Marx knew, for example, that superstructures, although determined in the last instance by the structures of social production, nevertheless have their own specific internal articulation and that, therefore, there can be no question of explaining the relationship between, for example, ideology and 'economic base' unless the system of representations which is the ideology is first understood in its own internal organization. This rules out, for example, the possibility of explaining ideologies on the basis of a one-to-one correlation between elements within ideological discourse and elements within the economic base.[13] Lévi-Strauss has frequently pointed out that his own work is a form of 'ideology analysis' and has made clear its coherence in this respect with Marx's theories.

Je ne postule pas une sorte d'harmonie préétablie entre les divers niveaux de structure. Ils peuvent être parfaitement—et ils sont souvent—en contradiction les uns avec les autres, mais les modalités selon lesquelles ils se contredisent appartiennent toutes à un même groupe. C'est bien, d'ailleurs, ce qu'enseigne le matérialisme historique quand il affirme qu'il est toujours possible de passer, par transformation, de la structure économique ou de celle des rapports sociaux à la structure du droit, de l'art ou de la religion. Mais jamais Marx n'a prétendu que ces transformations fussent d'un seul type, par exemple que l'idéologie ne puisse que refléter les rapports sociaux, à la façon d'un miroir. Il pense que ces transformations sont dialectiques, et, dans certains cas, il se donne beaucoup de mal pour retrouver la transformation indispensable qui semblait, au premier abord, rebelle à l'analyse.[14]

The requirement of specificity does not rule out the possibility that the different sciences may be integrated at a later stage of development. In fact it is a precondition for this. Cell theory and genetics are preconditions for molecular biology. Similarly the development of theories of sign systems (whether these be the ideologies discussed by Marx or by Lévi-Strauss, or those discussed by Barthes in *Mythologies*, or whatever) is necessary before any ambition to produce a 'totalized' theory of society or culture can hope for fulfilment. In the writings of Lévi-Strauss the distinction between nature and culture at first appears, in early works on kinship, as an ontological distinction. In his later work it reappears as a methodological distinction which coexists with a powerful reductionist faith. Social anthropology, says Lévi-Strauss, harbours a secret dream; 'elle appartient aux sciences humaines, son nom le proclame assez; mais, si elle se résigne à faire son purgatoire auprès des sciences sociales, c'est qu'elle ne désespère pas de se réveiller parmi les sciences naturelles, à l'heure du jugement dernier.'[15] One can be sure, however, that the science in which an integration is achieved of 'basic' and superstructural aspects of society, and all of this with the biological and the natural sciences, will be quite different from any existing science not only in its theory of society but also in its theory of material and biological systems. As Marx wrote: 'History itself is an *actual* part of *natural history*, of nature's development into man. Natural science will in time include the science of man as the science of man will include natural science: there will be *one* science.'[16]

The second general point I want to make concerning fundamental theoretical innovation is that a new theory may necessitate a critique of the 'empirical facts': '. . . pour atteindre le réel il faut d'abord répudier le vécu'.[17] This is a consequence of the principle that coherence is of the order of theory and not of fact. A theory may require us to use new criteria for deciding, in relation to observed phenomena, which are to be taken as the same, or similar to, each other, and which different. For example, it is a general feature of empirical taxonomies, in which classes are constructed on the basis of observed relations of affinity, that they always require revision in the light of a theory which serves to explain the relations between the entities being classified. Darwinian theory, in which taxonomic relations are interpreted in terms of 'propinquity of descent', necessitates a revision of pre-Darwinian taxonomies. Similarly Lévi-Strauss contests Tylor's classification of cultural artifacts. '. . . la fourchette européenne et la fourchette polynésienne, réservée aux repas rituels, ne forment pas davantage une espèce que les pailles à travers lesquelles le consommateur aspire une citronnade à la terrasse d'un café, la "bombilla" pour boire le maté, et les tubes à boire utilisés, pour des raisons magiques, par certaines tribus américaines.'[18]

Not only may relations between entities need to be re-evaluated in the light of theory but it can also happen that the entities themselves need to be identified differently. The interest of this lies in the fact that there is often something so compelling about the way in which our experience of the world is organized that this can actually constitute an important epistemological obstacle to the development of theories or to their acceptance. Distinctions or identities may be so deeply embedded in our discourse and thought about the world, whether this be because of their role in our practical lives, or because they are cognitively powerful and are an important aspect of the way in which we appear to make sense of our experience, that the theoretical challenge to them can be quite startling. This was probably the case, for example, with the way in which distinctions were drawn between relative and absolute motion, and between terrestrial and celestial phenomena until the seventeenth century, and much of Galileo's argument in his *The Two Chief World Systems* was designed to contest and replace these fundamental distinctions.[19] There are many cases of the same kind in the work of Lévi-Strauss. One might refer to his re-identification of the 'unit of kinship'. The structure which is the most elementary form of kinship rests, according to Lévi-Strauss, upon four terms (brother, sister, father, and son). It is the presence of the brother here that enables him to solve with elegance and economy the 'problem of the maternal uncle' by relating it directly to the operation of the incest taboo interpreted as the basis of the system of the exchange of women. Now this 'atom of kinship' is quite different not only from that assumed by earlier anthropologists, but also from that which is present in our ordinary, unreflective thought about familial relations. Lévi-Strauss cites this definition of the elementary structure of kinship by Radcliffe-Brown:[20]

The unit of structure from which a kinship is built up is the group which I call an 'elementary family', consisting of a man and his wife and their child or children . . . The existence of the elementary family creates three special kinds of social relationship, that between parent and child, that between children of the same parents (siblings), and that between husband and wife as parents of the same child or children . . . The three relationships that exist within the elementary family constitute what I call the first order.

One can see how the anthropologist's concepts here have been taken over from ordinary Western life. That the 'biological family' is the 'natural unit' of kinship is not simply an 'assumption' we make but is a way of organizing our inter-subjective, social experience which is thoroughly integrated with all aspects of our lives. Our cognitive, practical, emotional, and even political lives are all involved here, everything from the way we design our houses, assign responsibilities for the upbringing of our children, to the way in which we define prohibited and permissible sexual relationships. It is one of the conditions underlying many of our moral attitudes (as can be seen when it is contested at the practical level in various experiments in other forms of 'communal living'). It would probably be necessary to understand the articulation of these various systems of meaning and the conditions which render them possible and coherent before any serious discussion of the nature of moral principles or of moral argument could be attempted.[21] Thus this requirement of a 'repudiation of experience', which seems benign enough when what is in question is the classification of living organisms or the technicalities of research on the cultures of distant tribes, can in other cases meet a great deal of resistance to the extent that we may be required to practise the critique on the categories of our ordinary and familiar language. Science may invite us to give up ways of organizing our experience that seem to us so clearly correct, so forcefully guaranteed by what we know of the world by our ordinary experience of it that we might prefer to think of our world as falsifying the theory rather than have the theory disrupt our relations with the world. But there is no reason to believe that the opinions of philosophy or of commonsense have prima facie epistemological priority over those based on scientific theory. Is rest to count as fundamentally different from motion or only as a particular value of it? Should we abandon our ordinary ways of deciding which kinds of behaviour to think of as sexual in the light of psycho-analytic theory? Is Freud's claim that there is no fundamental difference between the structures and forces producing the manifestations of neurosis and those producing 'normal, healthy' activity refuted by the 'obvious fact' that the mad are different from the sane?[22] In any such cases it would be quite unjustifiable to have any great confidence in the distinctions and descriptions we are used to employing, in the ways we have of 'making sense of the world'. If theories demand startling reinterpretation of the world with which we are apparently familiar this is not necessarily because those theories are false. Another possibility is that our familiarity with the world is based on illusions.

It is always possible, then, that the sciences, and the human sciences in particular, will directly or indirectly threaten to disrupt philosophy by suggesting a re-evaluation of distinctions and concepts which play an important part in philosophical discussion. This was certainly dramatically the case in the scientific revolution of the seventeenth century. No area of philosophical inquiry was left untouched by the development of modern physics. It is as likely to be equally true of the developing human sciences. There is no doubt that these are as yet still relatively immature and are still struggling to articulate their fundamental discoveries. But it would be, in my opinion, a rash philosopher who decided to embark upon an investigation concerning the nature of historical explanation, the meaning of human freedom, the foundations of the moral life, or the problem of man as a subject of scientific inquiry, without first equipping himself for the task by reading and understanding *Capital*, *The Interpretation of Dreams*, and *The Elementary Structures of Kinship*.

Of course it is quite possible for science to be confused about the meaning of its own innovations. Philosophical argument has been influenced through and through by the development of science but this is not because science simply solves philosophical problems. Newtonian physics, quantum mechanics, and structural linguistics all suggest interpretations of such terms as 'law', 'determinism', and 'freedom'. Such terms are not terms within scientific theories and these theories do not in themselves constitute sufficient conditions for a clear understanding of such problems as that of the nature and extent of human freedom. But a philosophical discussion of such a problem cannot afford to ignore such theories because the interpretation of these terms is clearly dependent on, even if it is not given exhaustively by, the theoretical insights of the sciences. In the 'Finale' of *L'Homme nu* Lévi-Strauss strongly rejects any attempt by philosophy to exclude science from the study of man, or to legislate *a priori* as to what in man is appearance and illusion and what reality:

> A la suite des sciences physiques, les sciences humaines doivent se convaincre que la réalité de leur objet d'étude n'est pas tout entière cantonnée au niveau où le sujet la perçoit. Ces apparences recouvrent d'autres apparences qui ne valent pas mieux qu'elles, et ainsi de suite jusqu'à une nature dernière qui chaque fois se dérobe, et que sans doute nous n'atteindrons jamais. Ces niveaux d'apparence ne s'excluent pas, ne se contredisent pas les uns les autres, et le choix qu'on fait de chacun ou de plusieurs répond aux problèmes qu'on se pose et aux propriétés diverses qu'on veut saisir et interpréter. Libre au politique, au moraliste et au philosophe d'occuper l'étage jugé par eux seul honorable et de s'y barricader, mais qu'ils ne prétendent pas y enfermer tout le monde avec eux et interdire, pour s'attaquer à des problèmes distincts des leurs, d'agir sur la tourelle du microscope, changer le grossissement, et faire ainsi apparaître un objet autre derrière celui dont l'exclusive contemplation les ravit.[23]

In particular any nostalgia or humanism which leads philosophy to insist on the subjective and the individual over the unconscious and the social, as either having epistemological priority or as being the determinants of meaning in our lives, is failing in its duty to enter into serious dialogue with science, and in the commitment to truth which is their common concern.

That theory may require a reinterpretation of fact may have particularly drastic consequences, then, in those sciences of which the subject-matter is the contents of conscious human experience. The domain of subjectivity has been taken in philosophy, and, I dare say, also in commonsense, to be characterized by a particular epistemological status. It does not seem possible to throw doubt on our knowledge of the content of our subjective experience or on the fact of the existence of the subject whose experience it is. The relationship between the subject (the knower) and his subjective experiences (the known) seems to have epistemological inviolability because this is not, as is the case of our relationship with objects in the physical world, a relationship of exteriority, in which alien, transcendent objects are always, as it were, known only 'at a distance'. The meaning and identity of wishes, intentions, percepts, sensations, and so on can, it has been thought, be known with certainty because this meaning has its origin in the subject himself. It once seemed that it could not make sense to talk about intentions and desires which are unconscious, which are the meaning of a person's actions, and yet of which he is himself unaware and even strongly repudiates. Structuralism, and also some modern philosophy, challenges this priority of the subject and any 'philosophy of consciousness' which is based on it.

This introduction of doubt into a domain which may have seemed immune to it appears at both a theoretical and a practical level. Consider, for example, the actual practice of anthropological investigation. It has often been suggested that an obstacle to the study of man arises from the general fact that observation of an object is inevitably an interaction with it, and thereby must cause a transformation of its state. In many cases this interference is of no consequence, since the scale of the change produced by the observation is quite negligible compared to that of the values which are being observed. But people are like electrons in this respect, that they are extremely sensitive to being observed, and there is no way of being certain that what is observed is not an artefact of the investigation itself. While this is no doubt the case, and may on occasion be of great importance, it is the consequence of the inquiry on the observer himself, rather than on the object of his inquiry, which is of such importance and interest in anthropology (and also, of course, in psycho-analysis, literary studies, and so on). The process of observation is also a process of self-observation. 'Dans l'expérience ethnographique, par conséquent, l'observateur se saisit comme son propre instrument d'observation.'[24] In his tribute to Rousseau, 'founder of the sciences of man', Lévi-Strauss explains why this confrontation and interaction with others have as their first consequence not knowledge but doubt, and specifically self-doubt. The anthropologist who takes his informants seriously as men, and thereby fundamentally as a reflection of what he himself is (and while this may be a precondition of understanding them it is clearly by no means a necessary consequence of meeting and being with them), is confronted, paradoxically, with the totally alien. Not only does he discover behaviour and institutions which he has no way of 'reading', of assigning meanings to. More importantly he realizes that he can gain no access to these meanings simply through his knowledge of the subjective interpretations offered by his informants. He comes to see the gap between subject and meaning, just as it is revealed, in a quite different situation, to the psycho-analyst whose problem is defined by his recognition that his patients do not know what they are doing and do not understand the speech and symbols which obsess and dominate them and through which they live. The coherence of meaning is revealed as inaccessible to the subject and alien to him; not only to the anthropologist but also to those who are what they are in and through these meanings, and who have no immediate sense of the 'questionableness' of what they do. This must also be the discovery of the alien, of the 'other', in oneself, the realization of the presence of the unconscious. Thus this is, for the observer, something far more radical than simply the recognition of the 'relativity' of his own values and attitudes. It is not simply a matter of the problem, much discussed in Anglo-American philosophy, of the bias of the observer, of his obligation not to allow himself to read a strange text as if it were written in his own language. It involves not just 'bracketing' one's own values, but recognizing their source and thus their otherness and their opaqueness.

Ce que Rousseau exprime, par conséquent, c'est—vérité surprenante, bien que la psychologie et l'ethnologie nous l'ait rendue plus familière—qu'il existe un 'il' qui se pense en moi, et qui me fait d'abord douter si c'est moi qui pense. Au 'que sais-je?' de Montaigne (d'où tout est sorti), Descartes croyait pouvoir répondre que je sais que je suis, puisque je pense; à quoi Rousseau rétorque un 'que suis-je?' sans issue certaine, pour autant que la question suppose qu'une autre, plus essentielle, ait été résolue: 'suis-je?'; et que l'expérience intime ne fournit que cet 'il', que Rousseau a découvert et dont il a lucidement entrepris l'exploration.[25]

There are of course psychological dimensions to this experience (and it no doubt has much in common with the experience of the training analysis); but I am concerned here only with the peculiarity of the situation from the point of view of epistemology. The domain of subjectivity, in which we seem to discover both freedom and certainty, is revealed as a domain of representations governed by laws over which I have no control, and generating meanings which escape me. Thus the ethnologist's experience can be, paradoxically, an experience of recognition of myself in others and thereby of the other in myself. Doubt is a precondition of knowledge and the epistemological status of ethnology is such that, as Merleau-Ponty says, 'its uncertainty ends only if the man who speaks of man does not wear a mask himself.'[26] As Rousseau's *Confessions* were the product and logical consequence of his reflections on man so also *Tristes Tropiques* records the essential movement of self-doubt and reflection required by the commitment to ethnology.

Chaque fois qu'il est sur le terrain, l'ethnologue se voit livré à un monde où tout lui est étranger, souvent hostile. Il n'a que ce moi, dont il dispose encore, pour lui permettre de survivre et de faire sa recherche; mais un moi physiquement et moralement meurtri par la fatigue, la faim, l'inconfort, le heurt des habitudes acquises, le surgissement de préjugés dont il n'avait pas le soupçon; et qui se découvre lui-même, dans cette conjoncture étrange, perclus et estropié par tous les cahots d'une histoire personnelle responsable au départ de sa vocation, mais qui, de plus, affectera désormais son cours. Dans l'expérience ethnographique, par conséquent, l'observateur se saisit comme son propre instrument d'observation; de toute evidence, il lui faut apprendre à se connaître, à obtenir d'un *soi*, qui se révèle comme *autre* au *moi* qui l'utilise, une évaluation qui deviendra partie intégrante de l'observation d'autres soi. Chaque carrière ethnographique trouve son principe dans des 'confessions', écrites ou inavouées.[27]

This discovery of self-doubt at the practical level in the ethnological experience has its equivalent at the level of theory. As far as philosophy is concerned this has been located above all in attempts to liberate discussions of perception and of language from certain very general assumptions about knowledge and about speech. In particular I think that the phenomenology of Merleau-Ponty has a great deal in common, as far as its rejection of traditional accounts of meaning is concerned, with the basic insights of structuralism (although there is great difference in other respects). Merleau-Ponty, considered by many the most important of modern French philosophers, had a long and intimate relationship with the development of structuralist theory in France. He was among the first to grasp the importance of Saussure's *Cours de linguistique générale*, and his early work was heavily influenced by Gestalt psychology. He had many contacts with those who have subsequently become celebrated as structuralist theorists (whether or not they are content to be thought of as such) including Barthes and Lacan. He was a friend of Lévi-Strauss and his colleague at the Collège de France. Much of his major work of the last years of his life was dominated by his reflections on the philosophy of language and on psycho-analytic theory, in which he adopted a sympathetic but detached and critical position in relation to structuralism. The theoretical issues involved here, which are at present still very much at the centre of French philosophical life, and on which the debate has by now been prolonged and intense, are of great complexity, and I cannot attempt here even to summarize their content. I can only give an impressionistic and fragmentary account of some of the basic insights involved.

What is involved in my perception of an object or in my reference to an object in speech? The way in which we see and speak about objects is such as to mislead us systematically about the foundations of knowledge and language, and about where we must look in order to understand them. The very immediacy of the relation between the perceiving subject and that which he sees or that which he says, and the very familiarity of these performances make it extremely difficult to locate the mystery in the right place. Thus if I use the word 'table' in referring to an object of a particular kind I can become aware of this as something which demands explanation when I notice the 'gap' between the word and the object, when I realize that the relation which is established between them (the relationship of meaning between a word and a concept, or of reference between a phrase and an object) is not a relation established by nature, and is not guaranteed or sustained by the intrinsic properties of either of the items related. How then is the relation established and how is it sustained? Similarly, if I see a table and thereby know that it is a table, this must be because some relationship (in this case one of recognition) is involved between me, the subject, and that which I see. How is reference and how is recognition possible? The tendency is to suppose that they are possible by virtue of some relationship having been established in memory, or by habituation, between objects of particular kinds on the one hand, and particular words on the other. Thus, it might be said, I have learned to *associate* this word 'table' with objects which have particular properties, and it is this which allows me to identify particular objects as tables when I see them. So the relationship must be guaranteed ultimately by similarities between things, and it is this that allows continuity and coherence in speech about those things. Of course which associations I learn will depend on which language community I am brought up in, which language I learn to speak, and in this sense I am socially conditioned and my knowledge is socially determined.

But this account is profoundly misleading. One might say that it is based on a misidentification of the elementary units of speech and of knowledge, a misidentification which comes about by virtue of the way in which objects are constituted in the visual field and the way in which meanings are constituted within the structures of a language. It is as if it is possible for us to see and to speak only on condition that sight and speech in practice conceal the real relations out of which particulars are constructed. For in fact the particular object which I see is not simply recognized by me by virtue of its own set of observable properties, but is constructed in vision on the basis of its relations to other objects. My recognition of the table takes place against the background of an organization of the visual field. This spatial array of objects, which includes myself—for I am in the spatial field and am not contemplating it from outside—is not constructed out of any number of perceptions of particular objects, for each perception of a particular object presupposes it, is possible only on the basis of the presence of each of the others as a potential object of my perception. This can be put by saying that the object which I am looking at is a possible object of perception by virtue of the fact that it sustains two series of relationships with other objects, where these two series of relationships define the structure of the visual space in which it occupies a place. First there is an indefinite number of other objects which are substitutable for it in this place. Secondly, there are other objects which are combined with this one in the sense that they occupy other places in the space and my gaze can run over them, resting on them one by one, selecting them for particular attention, comparing them one with another. My recognition of an object is my familiarity, at an implicit, practical level, with a complex set of actual and visual relations which define the properties of a space.

Now this sketch of the foundations of visual meaning as sets of relationships of substitution and combination has a lot in common with accounts given in linguistics of meaning as 'diacritical'.

> What we have learned from Saussure is that, taken singly, signs do not signify anything, and that each one of them does not so much express a meaning as mark a divergence of meaning between itself and other signs. Since the same can be said for all other signs, we may conclude that language is made of differences without terms; or more exactly, that the terms of language are engendered only by the differences which appear among them.[28]

This insight is so much at variance with the way in which we think about meaning in commonsense, and its theoretical implications have proved to be so enormous, that it might be worth considering some further examples. If I stop my car at a red traffic light this is because, in the code for such signs, *red* means *stop*. This meaning cannot, of course, be traced back to any decision or choice on my part. And it is a meaning that I 'read' quite unreflectively, at the level of practical responses, without having to involve myself in conscious performances of interpretation, memory, association, or whatever. Meaning resides in, and gains its possibility from, practical social life. First of all the red light can have the meaning that it has only because in the situation in which I look for it there are only a limited number of possibilities. I am looking to see which colour or combination of colours is present in a situation where the code tells me in advance that a certain limited set of variations on the theme coloured lights is to be expected. The presence of the red is thus equally the absence of the green and the amber, it is not simply red *tout court*. Similarly in hearing someone speak English I am at each point in his speech listening for his selection of phonemes from a very limited set. To use an example from Jakobson, if I am introduced at a party to a Mr. Ditter I am able, quite without it occurring at the level of consciousness, to achieve a series of discriminations in which the differential value of each of the sound units making up the name are identified and synthesized into a word. My host did not say bitter or dotter or digger or ditty, but ditter. The possibility of this operation derives from my familiarity, at an operational or practical level, with the code in which this message is spoken. And this shows that the acquisition of a language such as that of the traffic lights is not achieved by learning piecemeal the meanings of the signs taken one by one and in isolation; it is the learning of a structured *system* within which each of the differential values finds its place. Red can only mean stop because green means go and because many other possibilities are ruled out as meaning nothing. Thus when I see the red light I see red-and-not-green. The performance I have been analysing breaks down and becomes impossible if I am confronted, in the place where I look for the signs, with unintelligible alternatives. If I look to see what colour the light is, and I find my eye coming to rest on a blue light, or on a red which is huge, or if the red and the green are alternating rapidly, then I not only see no intelligible light but I see the absence of the signs, the transgressing of the code. And as the world is now unfamiliar, so the nature of my performance in it will change, it being no longer possible for me to rely on my unreflective responses to its demands.

So each item is intelligible only by virtue of its relations with other actual or possible items, even though we are not explicitly conscious of these networks of relationships as we speak or hear a language. Another example of this that has proved to have important theoretical as well as practical consequences is discussed by Marx in *Capital*, namely the system of signs that constitutes the value-system in a society practising generalized commodity production. There are various levels of misidentification possible here. How is it possible for a coin or a commodity to have a value? We do not easily admit, perhaps, that we are confused into thinking that value resides in objects or coins or particular kinds of metal (although there is, I think, a great deal of fetishism of gold and silver which does not derive from their intrinsic aesthetic properties, but, in a confused way, from their location in the monetary system). We know that values are relations holding among series of exchangeable objects, and among monetary objects which can, as it were, stand proxy for them. But this system of value relationships is itself constituted within the system of relationships called wage–labour, which is a series of social relationships between men. It is only because men, as sources of certain amounts of labour–power, themselves appear as objects in exchange transactions, and because this system is generalized, that it is possible for there to be commodity production or the system of values within which consumption and exchange take place. No awareness of these structural relationships need be involved in any particular act of buying or selling even though they are the determining conditions of it. It is on the basis of such analyses that Lévi-Strauss concludes that 'le propre de la conscience est de se duper elle-même.' As Marx puts it in relation to this example:

> Hence, when we bring the products of our labour into relation with each other as values, it is not because we see in these articles the material receptacles of homogeneous human labour. Quite the contrary: whenever, by an exchange, we equate as values our different products, by that very act, we also equate, as human labour, the different kinds of labour expended upon them. We are not aware of this, nevertheless we do it. Value, therefore, does not stalk about with a label describing what it is. It is value, rather, that converts every product into a social hieroglyphic. Later on, we try to decipher the hieroglyphic, to get behind the secret of our social products; for to stamp an object of utility as a value, is just as much a social product as language.[29]

Both Merleau-Ponty and Lévi-Strauss attempt to go beyond such basic insights via the general question 'How are such systems of meaning possible?' Just how puzzling this is can only really be seen if one fully grasps the radical implications of their starting-point. In philosophical terms it can be put by saying that we are forced to reject any answer which presupposes the subject–object distinction. The world of objects, as it is thought in any particular language, is a product of that language, in the sense that its articulation is determined by that language. Different societies, cultures, and languages construct different worlds. In perception we are not acquainted with 'the world itself' but with the world as a semantic field, an endless series of 'messages', a world which is in its general forms familiar to me by virtue of the fact that both I and it are the products of the same culture. 'Notre perception . . . projette dans le monde la signature d'une civilisation, la trace d'une élaboration humaine' (Merleau-Ponty). We cannot say, therefore, that nature as we know it, whether in the form of a world perceived, or in the form of biological and physiological instincts, or in the form of the physical construction of our organs of perception, is a sufficient condition for the determination of any particular language or culture. For example the natural properties of objects and of light and of human perceptual organs do not, taken by themselves, determine a colour language; nor can they determine the organization of colour experience. Nor does our biological nature determine our sexual lives, for this also is a matter of life within systems of signification, based on the cultural articulation of the body as a semantic system and on the socially constituted space within which we mark off the permissible from the prohibited among possible objects of sexual attachment and possible manners of sexual expression.

Not only is it impossible to think an objective world as the source of systems of meaning, it is also impossible to identify this source as subjective. For there is not *first* a subject and a world, and then a language created at their point of contact. Because to *be* a subject is already to live in a world. It is very difficult to free ourselves from the metaphor of language as an instrument which a person can use in order to express feelings or communicate thoughts which have their source elsewhere. We tend to think of a person and the language in which he thinks and speaks as two independent things which come together for the purposes of social life. No doubt it is possible for a person to have 'wordless thoughts' but this is to miss the point. For to be a person is to live in a world. A 'wordless' thought which draws on that world for its images, or on the sounds and sights of that world for its inspiration, is precisely a 'cultured' thought (and is quite likely to be a simple and fleeting form of that thought on which myth and poetry are constructed). To have a world is to have acquired a culturally determined perceptual life, a language in which to think, an organization of intersubjective experience within which is possible one's particular style of affectivity and sexuality. Where there are yet no systems of meaning there can be no subject. 'L'homme parle donc, mais c'est parce que le symbole l'a fait homme' (Lacan).[30] Thus we cannot look for the determining conditions which make language and culture possible at the level of the subject. We cannot, in a Kantian manner, discover organizing powers of consciousness attributable to a transcendental subject. This is why Lévi-Strauss has accepted the description of his work as a 'Kantism without a transcendental subject' in which he searches for 'a combinative, categorizing unconscious, . . . a categorizing system unconnected with a thinking subject'.[31]

Thus the experienced world, and also those who experience it and attempt to render it intelligible in thought, are constituted within the complex systems of meaning which are human cultures. They do not exist independently of culture or prior to it, and, therefore, it cannot be in them that we shall be able to find an answer to the question of how culture is possible, or how speech is possible. In fact this may even seem to render any such inquiry fruitless, for where else might one look for an answer if neither to the object nor to the subject? It might also seem to rule out the possibility of human sciences, for where would we be able to locate necessary relations? We could hope to describe each particular system of meaning, or each group of such systems internally related by relations of isomorphism, as a system of necessary relations (in the form of rules of compatibility and exclusion and so on). But what could legitimize our aspiration to discover some principle of comparability among these systems, to discover the common ground on which systems of meaning are ultimately based? The answer given here by both structural anthropology and by phenomenology (although with quite different intentions) is that, having analysed the dichotomy between subject and object as derived or secondary we must look instead to that which is 'pre-subjective' in men and to that which is common to the world of all men. We must look for the way in which diverse languages, in which nature receives different expressions at the level of conscious meaning, are nevertheless based on a common pre-subjective function in men in a way that is implicitly 'authorized by nature'.

Behind the diversity of *langues*, and implicitly expressed in it, stand certain properties of the world and of the human mind. The ambition of Lévi-Strauss is not confined to searching out the formal properties of each particular system of meaning (or of groups of closely related systems) that are recoverable by ethnological research. The study of myth, for example, has as its aim the discovery of universal laws of thought in the form of a logic of sensible qualities: 'Au moyen d'un petit nombre de mythes empruntés à des sociétés indigènes qui nous serviront de laboratoire, nous allons effectuer une expérience dont, en cas de succès, la portée sera générale, puisque nous attendons d'elle qu'elle démontre l'existence d'une logique des qualités sensibles, qu'elle retrace ses démarches, et qu'elle manifeste ses lois.'[32] The study of myth should thus reveal how complex systems of conscious thought and expression arise on the basis of the presubjective symbolic function acting according to certain formal organizing rules (i.e. rules independent of particular contents) on the most general structures of the experienced world. These structures are present, however elaborated and covered over by thought in the course of its 'speculative enterprises', in the experience of all men.

Du monde, on ne peut dire purement et simplement qu'il est: il est sous la forme d'une asymétrie première, qui se manifeste diversement selon la perspective où l'on se place pour l'appréhender: entre le haut et le bas, le ciel et la terre, la terre ferme et l'eau, le près et le loin, la gauche et la droite, le mâle et la femelle, etc. Inhérente au réel, cette disparité met la spéculation mythique en branle; mais parce qu'elle conditionne, en deçà même de la pensée, l'existence de tout objet de pensée . . .

Le problème de la genèse du mythe se confond donc avec celui de la pensée elle-même, dont l'expérience constitutive n'est pas celle d'une opposition entre le moi et l'autre, mais de l'autre appréhendé comme opposition. A défaut de cette propriété intrinsèque—la seule, en vérité, qui soit absolument *donnée*—aucune prise de conscience constitutive du moi ne serait possible. N'étant pas saisissable comme rapport, l'être équivaudrait au néant. Les conditions d'apparition du mythe sont donc les mêmes que celles de toute pensée, puisque celle-ci ne saurait être que la pensée d'un objet, et qu'un objet n'est tel, si simple et dépouillé qu'on le conçoive, que du fait qu'il constitue le sujet comme sujet, et la conscience elle-même comme conscience d'une relation.[33]

The apparent similarity of this project of Lévi-Strauss to that of the philosopher Merleau-Ponty is very striking. The differences are, however, profound. It will not be possible here to do more than suggest the source of this divergence. Concerned to liberate philosophy from the classical opposition between subject and object Merleau-Ponty also starts from the fact that the system of signs that constitutes a language is only ultimately possible because of the manner of being of things in the world. In order for language to organize our perception of and thought about the world, the world must itself be organizable. What we can say of the world is that it is thinkable in many different languages because those languages, though diverse, are all responses to the same world, and express this fact in a way that is hidden from us even though we speak.

Le quadrillage sémantique opéré sur le monde perçu varie immensément d'une langue à une autre; mais on n'en trouvera pas une qui classe ensemble, sous le même mot, les roses d'hier matin et les étoiles de demain soir. On répète l'exemple des découpages différents du spectre visible par les langues, et des répertoires non congruents de couleurs qui en résultent. Exemple important, à condition d'en explorer toute la signification: la possibilité de découpages différents est fournie par la quasi-continuité du spectre visible, et deux fois plutôt qu'une. Il ne serait pas possible de le découper ainsi ou autrement s'il n'y avait pas une unité, aussi extra-linguistique, de l'être-coloré, si les couleurs ne tenaient pas ensemble: c'est le spectre visible qui est découpé. Il n'y aurait davantage possibilité de découpage arbitraire si le spectre n'était pas effectivement quasi-continu . . . Connaît-on une langue qui classe ensemble le museau d'un quadrupède et le tiers médian de sa queue? La relativité de la chose culturelle et langagière, par ailleurs incontestable, ne peut même pas être nommée sans que l'irrélativité, obscure et indicible, de la chose tout court ne soit immédiatement invoquée.[34]

This non-relativity, obscure and unspeakable, because it is that which makes all speech possible, is what Merleau-Ponty calls *l'être sauvage*.

All thought, including scientific thought, rests on this primary, pre-logical perceptual relationship with the world. But even though it is that which founds all perception it is not itself ever an object of perception, it cannot itself be perceived, for the characteristic of perception, as of speech, is that it comes about on the basis of a repression of this *perception sauvage*. It is the invisible in the visible. 'La clé est dans cette idée que la perception est de soi ignorance de soi comme perception sauvage, imperception.'[35] Phenomenological metaphysics takes as its paradoxical task the recovery of this relationship. This is at once its similarity and its fundamental difference from structuralism. For where the latter is 'the attempt to discover the pure forms that are imposed upon our unconscious before all content' the former is 'the endeavour to raise the ground of experience, the sense of being, the lived horizon of all our knowledge to the level of our discourse'.[36] This is also what produces the curious relationship between these two quite different inquiries, each thinking of the other as only a preliminary, as only pointing to the problem. For this grasp of *l'être sauvage* is, says Lévi-Strauss,[37]

à la fois la même chose et tout autre chose que ce que je devais moi-même appeler la pensée sauvage. D'accord avec Merleau-Ponty pour reconnaître que l'une et l'autre puisent 'à cette nappe de sens brut dont l'activisme ne veut rien savoir', je cherche la logique de ce sens, pour lui antérieur à toute logique. Ce qui, pour Merleau-Ponty, explique, ne fait, en somme pour moi qu'énoncer les données du problème, et délimiter le plan phénoménal à partir duquel il deviendra possible—et il s'agira—d'expliquer.

This difference of approach between the phenomenologist and the scientist might perhaps be clarified if we look at some of Lévi-Strauss's rather ambiguous remarks about science. He seems to argue for the view that there is no inherent superiority of science over other ways of making the world intelligible, such as magic and myth. Anxious to avoid ethnocentric prejudice he presents them as equally valid alternatives. In a startling passage in *Le Cru et le cuit* he writes: '. . . si le but dernier de l'anthropologie est de contribuer à une meilleure connaissance de la pensée objectivée et de ses mécanismes, cela revient finalement au même que, dans ce livre, la pensée des indigènes sud-américains prenne forme sous l'opération de la mienne, ou la mienne sous l'opération de la leur.'[38] 'La pensée sauvage', although an expression of universal laws of the mind, is not itself universal in the sense of being present in, or the basis of, all thought. It may also be that 'la pensée sauvage' can be found in all cultures. Science and 'la pensée sauvage' coexist in the same sense that science and art co-exist in our culture. It is not that the one is the foundation or necessary condition of the other. 'La pensée sauvage' is not primitive thought in the sense of a thought which is confined to people in whom we discover only the childhood of our species, and thus ensure that we do not recognize ourselves. It is 'neither the mind of savages nor that of primitive or archaic humanity, but rather mind in its untamed state as distinct from mind cultivated or domesticated for the purpose of yielding a return', and it survives in modern life both in art and in 'many as yet "uncleared" sectors of social life, where, through indifference or inability, and most often without our knowing why, primitive thought continues to flourish'.[39] An investigation of primitive thought, then, can hope to find, behind the apparent relativity of cultures, a certain generality of mind. Beneath the diversity of symbolic material and culture-relative rules for operations on this material anthropology might be able to discover some of the ways in which the powerful drive of the pre-subjective symbolic function is organized when it is with 'scrupulous attention directed entirely toward the concrete'.[40]

But for Merleau-Ponty coexistence is a more intimate relation. Science is itself grounded in 'la pensée sauvage' and the exploration of this relationship is essentially a philosophical task. Is it possible for science to take itself as the subject of its own inquiry, to question its own foundations? For Lévi-Strauss rational inquiry and that truth which is its goal are not themselves questioned. When science is compared with magic in *La Pensée sauvage* it is asserted that 'both approaches are equally valid.'[41] But this is a conjuring trick. For while it may be true that 'primitive thought' renders the world 'intelligible', science aims at something different from this; it aims not just at 'intelligibility' in the sense given to this notion here by Lévi-Strauss, but at truth. From this perspective it is forced to regard magic, 'valid' or not, practically effective or not, as *false*, since it is built around relationships discovered at the level of the sensible and it is not, as it happens, at this level that the truths at which science aims are to be found. In as much as primitive thought does something more than, or different from, that achieved by science, it is that which, as Lévi-Strauss himself elsewhere remarks, is to be found in our culture in such enterprises as that of art, and I should add, of metaphysics. 'We must not simply say that philosophy is compatible with sociology, but that it is necessary to it as a constant reminder of its tasks . . . Giving up systematic philosophy as an explanatory device does not reduce philosophy to the rank of an auxiliary or a propagandist in the service of objective knowledge; for philosophy has a dimension of its own, the dimension of coexistence.'[42] And if this philosophy is, as Lévi-Strauss says of ritual, 'un jeu compliqué et dans son essence irrationnel',[43] this is so because it seeks to capture the contradiction, which is necessarily repressed by science, that is the coexistence of life and thought. 'La pensée sauvage' is not replaced by science as Lévi-Strauss seems to indicate, but coexists with it as its foundation. And it is for philosophy to recall to science the presence of this contradiction by pointing to its manifestations at the heart of science itself—for example in the coexistence of signified and signifier, or in the nature of the diachrony as it is revealed in creative expression.[44] Just as the linguist cannot, as he speaks, replace the 'silent work of the body' which makes language possible with his own objective knowledge of it, so the scientist always lives, loves, and dies within the net of signifying systems which have their origin not in his rational contemplation of the world but elsewhere, in that which speaks through him, and in his being in the world.

NOTES

1. For recent discussions of this point see I. Lakatos and A. Musgrave (eds.), *Criticism and the Growth of Knowledge* (Cambridge University Press, Cambridge, 1970).
2. C. Lévi-Strauss, *The Scope of Anthropology* (Jonathan Cape, London, 1967), p. 20. Tr. of the French *Leçon inaugurale*, Collège de France, 5 Jan. 1960 (Paris, 1960), p. 17.
3. On the necessity for teleological explanation in kinship studies see Lévi-Strauss, 'The Future of Kinship Studies', *Proceedings of the Royal Anthropological Institute for 1965* (1965); on the use of mathematics in structural anthropology see Lévi-Strauss, *Anthropologie structurale* (Plon, Paris, 1958), ch. 3, and a much more important discussion in *L'Homme nu* (Plon, Paris, 1971), pp. 566–9.
4. *Anthropologie structurale*, p. 67. See also the *Leçon inaugurale*, p. 28 (*The Scope of Anthropology*, p. 32), where Lévi-Strauss explains the connection between the method of transformations and the fact that his science is concerned with meanings.
5. *Leçon inaugurale*, p. 27. *The Scope of Anthropology*, p. 31: 'No science today can consider the structures with which it has to deal as being no more than a haphazard arrangement. That arrangement alone is structured which meets two conditions: that it be a system, ruled by an internal cohesiveness; and that this cohesiveness, inaccessible to observation in an isolated system, be revealed in the study of transformations, through which the similar properties in apparently different systems are brought to light.'
6. See *Le Cru et le cuit* (Plon, Paris, 1964), pp. 13–14.
7. *Leçon inaugurale*, p. 8. *The Scope of Anthropology*, p. 10: 'Durkheim was probably the first to introduce the requirement of specificity into the sciences of man, thereby opening the way for a renovation from which most of these sciences, and especially linguistics, benefited at the beginning of the twentieth century. In all forms of human thought and activity, one cannot ask questions regarding nature or origin before having identified and analysed phenomena and discovered to what extent their interrelations suffice to explain them. It is impossible to discuss an object, to reconstruct the process of its coming into being without knowing first *what it is*; in other words, without having exhausted the inventory of its internal determinants.'
8. E. B. Tylor, 'Anthropology', *Encyclopaedia Britannica*, 9th ed. (1875).
9. E. B. Tylor, *Primitive Culture*, cited in *Anthropologie structurale*, p. 6.
10. *Anthropologie structurale*, p. 6. Translation (*Structural Anthropology* (Allen Lane, London, 1968), p. 4): '... Nothing is more dangerous than this analogy. For even if the concept of species should be discarded once and for all in the development of genetics, what made—and still makes—the concept valid for the natural historian is the fact that a horse indeed begets a horse and that, in the course of a sufficient number of generations, *Equus caballus* is the true descendant of *Hipparion*.

The historical validity of the naturalist's reconstructions is guaranteed, in the final analysis, by the biological link of reproduction. An ax, on the contrary, does not generate another ax. There will always be a basic difference between two identical tools, or two tools which differ in function but are similar in form, because one does not stem from the other; rather, each of them is the product of a system of representations.'

11. *Anthropologie structurale*, p. 62. 'Because they are symbolic systems, kinship systems offer the anthropologist a rich field, where his efforts can almost (and we emphasize the "almost") converge with those of the most highly developed of the social sciences, namely, linguistics. But to achieve this convergence, from which it is hoped a better understanding of man will result, we must never lose sight of the fact that, in both anthropological and linguistic research, we are dealing strictly with symbolism. And although it may be legitimate or even inevitable to fall back upon a naturalistic interpretation in order to understand the emergence of symbolic thinking, once the latter is given, the nature of the explanation must change as radically as the newly appeared phenomenom differs from those which have preceded and prepared it' (*Structural Anthropology*, p. 51).
12. *Anthropologie structurale*, p. 61. 'Of course, the biological family is ubiquitous in human society. But what confers upon kinship its sociocultural character is not what it retains from nature, but rather, the essential way in which it diverges from nature' (*Structural Anthropology*, p. 50).
13. See J. K. Mepham, 'The Theory of Ideology in *Capital*', *Radical Philosophy*, ii (May 1972).
14. *Anthropologie structurale*, pp. 365–6. 'I do not postulate a kind of preexistent harmony between the different levels of structure. They may be —and often are—completely contradictory, but the modes of contradiction all belong to the same type. Indeed, according to dialectical materialism it should always be possible to proceed, by transformation, from economic or social structure to the structure of law, art, or religion. But Marx never claimed that there was only one type of transformation—for example, that ideology was simply a "mirror image" of social relations. In his view, these transformations were dialectical, and in some cases he went to great lengths to discover the crucial transformation which at first sight seemed to defy analysis' (*Structural Anthropology*, p. 333 (slightly modified)).
15. *Leçon inaugurale*, p. 27. *The Scope of Anthropology*, p. 31: 'It belongs to the human sciences, as its name adequately proclaims; but if it resigns itself to a period in purgatory beside the social sciences, it is because it does not despair of awakening among the natural sciences when the last trumpet sounds.' Cf. *The Savage Mind* (Weidenfeld and Nicolson, London, 1962), ch. 9: 'The opposition between nature and culture to which I attached much importance at one time now seems to be of primarily methodological importance.' And: '. . . I believe the ultimate goal of the human sciences to be not to constitute, but to

dissolve man.' Such arguments as this between reductive and dialectical materialism are not, of course, situated within the theoretical discourse of the sciences—they are philosophical. The scientific content of social anthropology cannot by itself resolve the problem or even ensure that it can be given clear meaning.

16. K. Marx, 'Economic and Philosophical Manuscripts' in *Writings of the Young Marx on Philosophy and Society*, ed. L. D. Easton and K. H. Guddat (Anchor Books, Doubleday, New York, 1967), p. 312.
17. Lévi-Strauss, *Tristes tropiques* (Plon, Paris, 1955), p. 50.
18. *Anthropologie structurale*, p. 7. *Structural Anthropology*, p. 4: 'The European fork and the Polynesian fork (which is used in ritual meals) do not constitute a species, any more than do the straws through which one sips lemonade at a café, the "bombilla" to drink maté, and the drinking tubes used for ritual purposes by some American Indian tribes.'
19. See P. K. Feyerabend, 'Problems of Empiricism: Part 2', in R. Colodny (ed.), *University of Pittsburgh Series in the Philosophy of Science* (University of Pittsburgh, Pittsburgh, Pa.), iv (1970), 275–353.
20. Cited in *Anthropologie structurale*, p. 60.
21. If I am right about this it would throw very great doubt on the value of almost everything that passes for moral philosophy in England.
22. Cf. Freud: 'Whereas for most people "conscious" and "psychical" are the same, we have been obliged to *extend* the concept of "psychical" and to recognize something psychical that is not conscious.' And: 'Whereas other people declare that "sexual" and "connected with reproduction" (or if you prefer to put it more shortly, "genital") are identical, we cannot avoid postulating something sexual that is not genital and has nothing to do with reproduction.'
23. *L'Homme nu*, p. 570. 'The human sciences must realize, as have the physical sciences, that the reality of that which they study is not entirely restricted to the level at which it is perceived by the subject. These appearances conceal others, which are worth no more than they are, and this continues as far as some 'final nature' which always eludes us and which we shall no doubt never reach. These levels of appearance are not mutually exclusive, do not contradict each other, and the choice we make of one or several of them is determined by the questions we are interested in asking and by the various properties which we wish to understand and to interpret. Political thinkers, moralists, and philosophers are free to concern themselves with whichever level they judge to be uniquely worthy and to barricade themselves therein. But they cannot claim the right to subject everybody else to this confinement, or to prohibit others, interested in quite different problems, from adjusting the controls of the microscope, changing the magnification, thus causing another object to appear behind that the exclusive contemplation of which so delights them.'
24. Lévi-Strauss, 'Jean-Jacques Rousseau, fondateur des sciences de l'homme', in *Jean-Jacques Rousseau* (Neuchâtel, 1962), p. 241.
25. Ibid., p. 242. 'Thus what Rousseau asserts is—a truth which is sur-

prising although psychology and ethnology have made it more familiar to us—that there exists an "it" which thinks in me, and which makes me doubt whether it is I that think. To the "what do I know?" of Montaigne (from which everything sprang) Descartes thought himself able to reply that I know that I am, because I think; to which Rousseau's response is a "what am I?" to which there is no certain solution, inasmuch as the question assumes that another, prior question, has been answered: "am I?"; and inasmuch as inner experience provides us only with that "it" which Rousseau discovered and which, with great lucidity, he undertook to explore.'

26. Maurice Merleau-Ponty, 'From Mauss to Claude Lévi-Strauss', in *Signs* (Northwestern University Press, Evanston, Ill., 1964), p. 120.
27. *Jean-Jacques Rousseau*, p. 241. 'Each time that he is in the field the ethnologist finds himself in a world where everything is foreign, and often hostile, to him. He has now only this "I" to rely on for survival and in conducting his research. But it is an "I" physically and morally battered by fatigue, hunger, discomfort, by the jarring of acquired habits and the upsurge of prejudices of which he had been completely unaware; and which discovers itself, in this alien predicament, crippled and incapacitated by all the vicissitudes of a personal history which was responsible, in the first place, for his vocation, and which will, moreover, from now on affect its course. Thus in the ethnographic experience the observer grasps himself as his own instrument of observation. Obviously he must learn to know himself, he must achieve an evaluation of a *self* which reveals itself to the "I" who uses it as *other*, and which must become an integral part of the observation of other selves. Each ethnographic career finds its principle in "confessions" either written or unacknowledged.'
28. Merleau-Ponty, 'Indirect Language and the Voices of Silence', in *Signs*, p. 39.
29. K. Marx, *Capital* (Foreign Languages Publishing House, Moscow, 1961), i. 74.
30. Jacques Lacan, *Écrits* (Seuil, Paris, 1966), p. 276.
31. *Le Cru et le cuit*, p. 19.
32. Ibid., p. 1. *The Raw and the Cooked* (Harper and Row, New York, 1970), p. 1: 'Using a small number of myths taken from native communities which will serve as a laboratory, I intend to carry out an experiment which, should it prove successful, will be of universal significance, since I expect it to prove that there is a kind of logic in sensible qualities, and to demonstrate the operation of that logic and reveal its laws' (slightly modified).
33. *L'Homme nu*, p. 539. 'Of the world one cannot say purely and simply that it is. It is under the form of an original asymmetry, which is manifested diversely depending on the perspective from which one apprehends it: between high and low, sky and earth, land and water, near and far, left and right, male and female, etc. Inherent in reality it is this disparity which sets mythic speculation going. But this is so because it conditions, even within thought, the existence of every object of

thought . . . The problem of the genesis of myth is thus inseparable from the problem of that of thought itself, of which the constitutive experience is not that of an opposition between the self and other, but of the other apprehended as opposition. In the absence of this intrinsic property—the only one, in fact, which is absolutely *given*—no constitutive act of consciousness in which the self could be grasped would be possible. Were Being not apprehendable as relation, it would be equivalent to non-Being [le néant]. The conditions for the appearance of myth are thus the same as for all thought, since thought can only be of an object, and any object, regardless of how simply or bare it is conceived, can only be such in that it constitutes the subject as subject, and consciousness itself as consciousness of a relation.'

34. C. Castoriadis, 'Le Dicible et l'indicible', *L'Arc*, xlvi (1971), 70. 'The semantic mapping which is operated upon the perceived world varies immensely from one language to another. But one will not find a single one which classifies together, under the same word, yesterday morning's roses and tomorrow evening's stars. The example of differences between languages in their dividing up of the visible spectrum, and the non-congruent colour-systems which result, is often cited. And this an important example as long as its full meaning is explored. The possibility of these differences of division is given by the fact of the quasi-continuity of the visible spectrum, and this in two ways. It would not be possible to effect a division in any particular way were it not for an extra-linguistic unity in the being of colour [de l'être-coloré], the fact that colours "belong together". It is the visible spectrum which is divided up. Moreover, there would be no possibility of arbitrary divisions if the spectrum were not in fact quasi-continuous . . . Do we know of any language which classifies together the muzzle of a quadruped and the middle third of its tail? The relativity of the cultural and linguistic world, although incontestable, cannot even be expressed without the obscure and unspeakable irrelativity of the world itself being immediately invoked.'
35. Merleau-Ponty, *Le Visible et l'invisible* (Gallimard, Paris, 1964), p. 266.
36. M. Foucault, *The Order of Things* (Tavistock, London, 1970), p. 299. Tr. of the French *Les Mots et les choses* (Gallimard, Paris, 1966).
37. 'De quelques rencontres', *L'Arc*, xlvi (1971), 45. '. . . At the same time both the same and something quite different from that which I was myself to call "la pensée sauvage". While agreeing with Merleau-Ponty that both [phenomenology and structuralism] draw upon "that layer of raw meaning [sens brut] of which activism wishes to know nothing", I am looking for the logic of this meaning, while it is for him anterior to all logic. That which, for Merleau-Ponty, is explanatory, for me does no more than state the terms of the problem, and delimit the phenomenal level from which it will become possible—and this will be our task—to explain.'
38. *Le Cru et le cuit*, p. 21. '. . . If the final aim of anthropology is to contribute to a better knowledge of objectified thought and its mechanisms, in the last analysis it would come to the same thing whether, in

this book, the thought of the South American Indians took shape through the operation of my thought, or mine through the operation of theirs.' The claim that mythical thought and scientific thought are not to be thought of as 'two stages or phases in the evolution of knowledge' and that 'both approaches are equally valid' is in *The Savage Mind*, p. 22.

39. *The Savage Mind*, p. 219. The passage reads in full: 'We are better able to understand today that it is possible for the two to co-exist and interpenetrate in the same way that (in theory at least) it is possible for natural species, of which some are in their savage state and others transformed by agriculture and domestication, to co-exist and cross, although—from the very fact of their development and the general conditions it requires—the existence of the latter threatens the former with extinction. But, whether one deplores or rejoices in the fact, there are still zones in which savage thought, like savage species, is relatively protected. This is the case of art, to which our civilization accords the status of a national park, with all the advantages and inconveniences attending so artificial a formula; and it is particuarly the case of so many as yet "uncleared" sectors of social life, where, through indifference or inability, and most often without our knowing why, primitive thought continues to flourish.'
40. Ibid., p. 220.
41. Ibid., p. 22.
42. Merleau-Ponty, 'The Philosopher and Sociology', in *Signs*, pp. 110, 113.
43. *L'Homme nu*, p. 608.
44. See Jacques Derrida, 'La Structure, le signe et le jeu dans le discours des sciences humaines', in *L'Écriture et la différence* (Seuil, Paris, 1967); and C. Castoriadis, art. cit.

# 7 'Structure' in Mathematics

ROBIN GANDY

THE purpose of this paper is to describe and discuss the notion of 'abstract structure' as it occurs in mathematics. I shall also consider briefly some of the uses and abuses of this notion by those who are interested in structuralism.

Mathematicians are more interested in ideas than in facts, more attracted to the general and the abstract than to the particular and the concrete. Further, they always seek to escape from nebulosity and confusion to clarity and precision; from romantic mists to classical sunlight. These preoccupations may lead to oversimplification and triviality; indeed there is a sense in which the definition of structure which we shall give is a trivial one. But it would be as well before going further to scotch some misapprehensions. It is true that large parts of pure mathematics consist of conclusions which can be derived by simple logical rules from given definitions and axioms. (In the early days of logical positivism such conclusions were sometimes misleadingly referred to as tautologies.) And this fact may give rise to the impression that mathematicians are concerned with obtaining trivial results by mechanical methods, an impression which experience may support since, indeed, most school mathematics is concerned with purely mechanical operations. But the impression is totally misleading. First there is a theorem (Church's theorem for the predicate calculus) which says that although there is a mechanical way of *generating*, one by one, the logical consequences of a given set of axioms, yet there is no mechanical way of deciding whether *or not* a given statement will ever be generated in this way—i.e. whether or not it is a theorem of the particular branch of mathematics considered. Secondly, mathematicians do not normally proceed by logical steps—

that process is much too cumbersome and slow; instead they form some kind of intuitive picture and seek to find their way about in it by insight and example. Thirdly the most creative mathematics consists not so much in exploring the consequences of given definitions and axioms, but in finding ones which will embody ideas at first only dimly perceived. Thus much of a worthwhile mathematical journey will be spent in a fog of incomplete analogies, half-worked-out examples, and hazy intuitions. By trial and error, by exploring blind alleys, by hard and imaginative thought, the mathematician finally emerges on the sunlit summit. The clouds disperse and a direct route is seen and retraced. Traditionally—though perhaps wrongly—the published account describes only this direct route; the gropings and false trails are ignored.

But, to return from this digression, it is the clear view and the well-marked path which the mathematician seeks. And some of the leading structuralists (in particular, Chomsky and Lévi-Strauss) are like the mathematician in this respect. But structuralism also has its wilder shores: I cannot resist quoting a message from one of them:[1]

> But he [Piaget] also discards the whole possibility of a *certain* play of differences which would inhabit the formal set of relationships and make it evolve towards a certain complex entailment of Heraclitean discontinuity. One realises how this recognition of the relationship of a set of non-Aristotelian premises to structuralist 'reason' can be a key point or a test case. It is one point where a crisis of structuralist rationality emerges: how far is structuralism able to integrate *otherness*?

There is a fog from which I see no escape.

Now to work. Fig. 1 is an example of a structure—the relations of love and marriage between certain people. The facts are vouched for by Iris Murdoch in her interesting anthropological study *A Severed Head*.[2]

I have selected from the wealth of material provided by Miss Murdoch certain properties and relations: sex, marriage, love, and kinship. The concentration on particular aspects of a situation is one of the characteristic features of structuralism. There is an extreme form of holistic philosophy which asserts that everything depends on everything else; that one cannot get at the truth without knowing all about everything; that nothing is irrelevant. This point of view may provide a starting-point for mystical contemplation, but it prohibits rational inquiry. In the first place our information is always partial; we simply do not know

> . . . who fished the murex up,
> What porridge had John Keats.*

Secondly, our brains cannot cope with too much information. We *must* select what is relevant to our purpose; of course there will often be controversy about what is and what is not relevant. My purpose is expository, so I have selected as much as will make a nice diagram; I have left out, for example, the time factor. I have left in the names for the sake of comparison with the book. From an anthropological

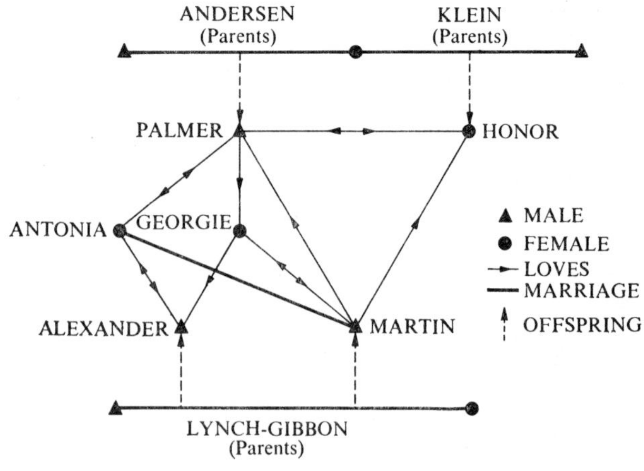


FIG. 1

point of view they would be irrelevant. (Wilhelm Stekel, however, once published a psycho-analytic study to show how people's lives were influenced by their names; but when taxed with betraying the confidence of his patients he admitted that he had made up the names.)

But what this article is about is mathematics, not anthropology. Hence the *nature* of the relations is also irrelevant; the abstract or mathematical structure is completely represented by Fig. 2. What this shows is a *pattern of relationships*; no interpretation is specified. We can make up other, seemingly dissimilar situations which will

* But we do know what porridge Guy Burgess had; according to Goronwy Rees (in *A Chapter of Accidents*) it contained kippers and garlic.

exhibit the same pattern. For example we might replace the 'people' by rectangular rubber sponges, blue (for triangular), and pink (for circle). The marriage relation is to be represented by contact along a vertical face (with children depending from it); the love relation by contact along a horizontal face, with the lover on top (so that mutual love would involve two contacts). Actually to realize this interpretation would probably require extreme physical contortions, the cutting of lugs and holes; I shall leave its construction to the reader and call it Fig. 3. I have introduced it only to emphasize that situations which *look* very different may nevertheless have the same structure. With respect to the given relations, the situation described in the book (Fig. 1), and Figs. 2 and 3 all exhibit the *same* structure; they are, in

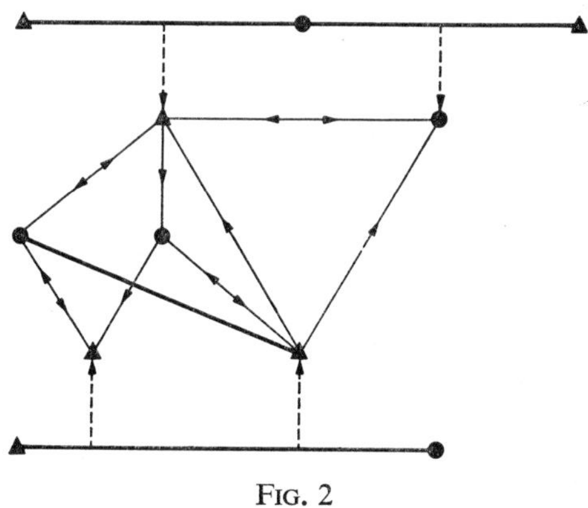

FIG. 2

mathematical language, *isomorphic*. This indifference to the form of *representation* is what Bertrand Russell referred to when he said that in mathematics we are not interested in what we are talking about.

This example is of a 'first-order' relational structure; certain objects are given together with certain relations between them. (For simplicity we count properties as (one-term) relations.) In more complex situations we may, first, wish to use functions. This would be the case if we had considered the *history* of *A Severed Head*—the relations would then appear as functions of time. However, it is always possible to represent a function as a relation between its arguments. Secondly, we may be forced to consider relations of higher order (or *type*); that is relations between relations, properties of such relations, and so on. For example, a follower of Lévi-Strauss might say 'roast is to boiled as giving is to keeping.' In the history of mathematics there is a steady progress up the hierarchy of types or orders. Greek mathematics was primarily concerned with points and numbers (real, rational, and integral) and the relations between them. Seventeenth- and eighteenth-century mathematics was mostly concerned with *functions* of real numbers and the relations between *them*. In the nineteenth century the calculus of variations led to the study of *functionals* (functions of functions). Today, in quantum mechanics and functional analysis one often has to consider functions of functions of functions. And in set theory one extends the hierarchy into the transfinite.

An abstract or mathematical structure then is specified by a domain of objects and a pattern of relations, relations of relations, etc., over the domain. Let me emphasize the abstractions involved. Firstly, the nature of the objects is of no importance; the objects are simply what the relations are between—in mathematical language, the objects appear only as arguments. In this way they are rather like Kant's 'things in themselves' but there is nothing mysterious about them; in particular they do not have essences. Like anti-holism, anti-essentialism is a distinctive feature of the structuralist approach. If some quality of an object is considered as vital to the understanding of the structure, then that quality (as it might be, the colour of Martin's eyes) must be listed among the relevant relations.

Secondly, the nature of the relations is also irrelevant; they are to be considered as given in extension. For a finite structure this can be done by listing which first-order relations hold between which objects, which (second-order) relations hold between which first-order relations, and so on. Our example, described in this way, would look like this:

*Md, Fc, Mk, Mp, Fh, Fa, Fg, Mm, Mx, Ml, Mn;*
*dWc, cWd, kWc, cWk, mWa, aWm, lWn, nWl;*
*pCdc, hCck, xCln, mCln;*
*pLh, hLp, aLp, pLa, pLg, mLp, mLh, aLx, xLa, gLx, gLm, mLg.*

FIG. 4

In the case of infinite structures, listing is not a practical procedure; but according to the most commonly accepted mathematical philosophy (Platonism or realism), one simply imagines that it can be done.

Finally, by using some boring technical devices, it is possible to portmanteau the given relations of various orders into a single relation of a sufficiently high order. A structure is then simply a domain of colourless individuals together with a single higher-order relation over it. This definition of mathematical structure, which enshrines ideas due to Cantor, Frege, Russell, and Zermelo, was first given by Bourbaki* in 1939.[3] Those who enjoy abstraction, generality, and simplicity may, at first encounter, think that this definition contains some powerful magic; one seems, as it were, to be able to hold untold complexity in the palm of one's hand. But the appearance is deceptive. The definition *is* neat, but it is also trivial, and if one starts detailing the 'untold complexity' of a particular structure it will soon spill out of one's hand. (Those readers who do not enjoy abstraction can ignore the definition and continue to think of a structure as a pattern of relations—for the rest of this paper that will do well enough.)

One of the ways in which the definition is trivial is that it makes no distinction between interesting, significant, or beautiful structures, and purely random assignments of relations between objects. This being 1972 I need not apologize for using 'pattern' to include totally chaotic arrangements; action painting, anti-art, *musique concrète*, and aleatory composition all work with this liberal notion of 'pattern'. There are people nowadays who think that disorder is more important than order. It is perhaps an interesting fragment of the history of ideas to observe that if I had been writing fifty years or more ago I should have had to labour this point. Russell, Eddington, and Carnap, in their writings on our knowledge of the external world, all show a tendency to believe that *any* structure must have a certain coherence and order. Indeed, in mathematics at least, this divergence of points of view was already quite clear in the early nineteenth century. There was considerable controversy about whether an 'arbitrary function' was given by an unspecified *rule*, or whether it could be wholly random.

I should emphasize that I am still discussing the *mathematical* concept of structure. It is of course one of the prime tenets of structuralism that the structures (of, for example, language, social codes,

* 'N. Bourbaki' is the pseudonym for a (gradually changing) group of predominantly French mathematicians. Their great and lengthy treatise (not yet complete) has had a profound effect on the mathematics of the last three decades.

artefacts, systems of thought) which human beings create are far from random and have a high degree of order; and that by studying this order we can discover universal truths about the human mind. Some authors (for example, Piaget in his book *Structuralism*)[4] have sought to place restrictions on the notion of 'structure' even in the most abstract contexts. But I think this is mistaken. We cannot be sure that a structure which does not satisfy the restrictions may not one day arouse great interest. Further, some of the conditions which Piaget imposes—in particular the condition of 'self-regulation'—look extremely artificial in a mathematical context.

But although the mathematician does not wish to exclude any structures from consideration, he naturally finds some structures more interesting than others; he would not find the structure of Figs. 1–4 particularly interesting. Before discussing what makes a structure interesting let me give some examples.

*Example 1.* The structure has two elements 0 and 1, and two functions (or operations) called 'plus' (+) and 'times' (.). The structure is completely described by the following equations:

$$0+0=0,\quad 0+1=1,\quad 1+0=1,\quad 1+1=0;$$
$$0\,.\,0=0,\quad 0\,.\,1=0,\quad 1\,.\,0=0,\quad 1\,.\,1=1.$$

This structure is both very old, and bang up to date. If we read '0' as 'even' and '1' as 'odd', then the above equations are just the laws of the Odd and the Even which were known to the Pythagoreans in the sixth century B.C., and are recorded in Book IX of Euclid. But also, as every modern schoolchild knows, the equations give the rules of binary arithmetic (without carry) as used by electronic computors. Further the structure is the simplest example of a finite number field; such structures were first investigated by Galois round about 1830, and play a fundamental role in the theory of equations, the theory of numbers, and algebraic geometry. Finally the structure is closely connected with the simplest Boolean algebra, and so has interpretations in the theory of sets and the propositional calculus.

*Example 2: Groups.* This is an example of a *kind* of structure. I shall not give a formal definition. A group can be thought of as a set of actions A, B, . . ., or operations which can be compounded together—do A and then do B. The resulting action must again be a member of the group; the process of compounding is usually called 'multiplication'. Inaction is to be counted as a member of the group (the identity or neutral element). Each action must be invertible, so that if one compounds an action with its inverse the result is inaction —one gets back to where one started. Finally the result of a sequence of actions may depend on the order in which they are performed, but must not depend on the order in which they are compounded. Thus 'do A and then do the result of compounding B followed by C' must have the same effect as 'do the compound of A followed by B and then do C'—either of these can then be simply read as 'do A, then B, then C'. Familiar examples of groups are provided by the rotations of a rigid body and the permutations of a set of objects. If you take A to be 'rotate clockwise through 90° about an axis running from east to west' and B to be 'rotate clockwise through 90° about an axis running from north to south' you will find that 'do A then B' does not give the same result as 'do B then A'. Note that I have described the actions by directions fixed in space, so that their description does not depend on the position of the body. This is necessary if the result of a sequence of actions is not to depend on the order of their compounding. To say that an object or situation is symmetrical in some respect is to say that it will look exactly the same after we have performed certain actions on it; for example, if we move an (infinite!) sheet of wallpaper through its repeat distance, then its appearance is unaltered. Given a symmetrical object the actions which leave the appearance unaltered will form a group; a classic example is the rotations which leave unaltered the appearance of a regular solid. Quite generally we can explore the symmetries of one of our abstract structures by considering the group of those permutations of the individuals which leave the structure looking the same. It turns out that not only is the study of groups a *possible* way of exploring symmetries but also a powerful and fruitful way of doing this. (The interested reader may consult H. Weyl's book *Symmetry*.)[5] This is the chief reason for the importance of group theory in the theory of mathematical and physical structures. (An example of its application to anthropological structures will be found in Andre Weil's appendix to Lévi-Strauss's *The Elementary Structures of Kinship*.[6] But some anthropologists, and this humble non-anthropologist, find highly implausible the assumptions which are necessary to produce the rather complex kinship structure considered.)

So far I have considered groups through their applications or representations. But it is easy to express them as abstract structures: as individuals we take the actions of the group, and we consider the single relation 'A is the result of compounding B followed by C'. The restrictions we imposed on this relation are in fact quite severe; for example, if $p$ is a prime number there is only one abstract group which has exactly $p$ elements. The richness and power of the theory of groups stem from this restrictiveness. In mathematics, as elsewhere, the return depends on the investment; feeble axioms will yield only feeble theorems.

There is a historical accident connected with the theory of groups which is of some importance for the development of structuralism. Group theory was one of the first mathematical theories to be presented purely abstractly, and certainly it was the most important. Two separate concrete isomorphic representations of a group (e.g. as a group of rotations and as a group of permutations) were taken as referring to the *same* abstract group. So people who learnt their mathematics round about 1900 tended to think of groups as the paradigm or even as the only example of abstract structures. In Chapter IX of *The Philosophy of the Physical Sciences*,[7] Eddington continually confuses 'abstract structure' with 'group'. Piaget, both in his earlier work on concept-formation and in his *Structuralism*, tries to dress up structures which are patently not groups in groups' clothing. I repeat that (as Fig. 2 illustrates) *any* structure can be presented as a purely abstract structure.

There are many considerations which combine to make mathematicians agree that certain structures, or sorts of structure are interesting: applicability, occurrence in disparate fields of study, comprehensibility, simplicity, beauty are some of them. I doubt that the question 'what makes a structure mathematically important?' can be answered in a philosophical, absolute way. History (the history of ideas) is sure to be relevant; our grandchildren will give answers different from ours. Bourbaki believe that there are certain 'mother structures' (*structures mères*) which are fundamental to all mathematics; but not everyone would agree with their choice of these.

Let us now consider what kinds of abstract structure occur in structuralist investigations in other fields. There are certainly interesting things to be said here about linguistic structures. But first, I should like to say something about anthropology. Except possibly for patterns of kinship (see pp. 48 ff. above), the *abstract* structures appear to be rather simple. For example, in the analysis of myths (as exemplified by Dr. Leach in his contribution to this volume) one considers one or several sequences of persons and events, and one categorizes the incidents in some fairly general way (e.g. as 'natural' or 'artificial'). By so doing one uncovers certain regular patterns or rhythms. For example, the incidents may alternate between two polarities; or two myths may exhibit the opposite polarities at corresponding points in time. The existence of these regular patterns is held to justify the analysis—in particular the regularity supports the belief that the categories or polarities chosen are fundamental to the type of thought which produced the myths. Since (as far as I am aware) the number of events in sequences actually considered and the number of beats in a 'bar' of the rhythm are small, it follows that the *abstract* structures considered are simple ones.

Hence the analysis is unlikely to tell us anything interesting about mathematical thought. What it should do is to confirm the significance of the chosen categories.

Finally we discuss the structures which are considered in structuralist linguistics. Although the sentences which occur in everyday use are fairly short, it is held that they are constructed according to rules which should be applied to the formation of sentences of arbitrary length. The structures determined by these rules *are* mathematically interesting. Indeed they involve a concept which is fundamental to mathematical thought; their study casts considerable light on the workings of the human mind.

The concept in question is *computability*. I shall first illustrate it by showing how the function $2^n$ can be computed on an abacus. This abacus will have three wires (or 'registers'), $A$, $B$, $C$. At any moment there will be a finite number (possibly zero) of beads on the right of each wire; these numbers are called the contents of the respective registers, and will be denoted by $\overline{A}$, $\overline{B}$, $\overline{C}$. On the left of each wire there is an indefinite supply of beads; in a single move the contents of each register can be increased or decreased by one by sliding a bead from left to right or right to left. The latter operation leads to a *conditional* instruction; if a register is empty we cannot perform it, and we must be told what to do instead. Initially the contents of $A$ is 1, that of $B$ is 0, and that of $C$ is $n$. We start with 'instruction number 1' and then proceed according to the following table (Fig. 5). The answer ($2^n$) is the contents of $A$ when the halt instruction is reached. Suppose that $n=0$, so that $\overline{C}=0$. Then instruction number 1 tells us to halt; the answer ($\overline{A}$) is 1, in accord with the mathematical convention $2^0=1$. If $n=1$, then we must perform successively the instructions 2, 3, 4 which have the effect of setting $\overline{A}=0$,

| *Instruction number* | *Register affected* | *Condition* | *Operation* | *Next instruction* |
|---|---|---|---|---|
| 1 | $C$ | $\neq 0$<br>$=0$ | $-1$<br>Halt | 2 |
| 2 | $A$ | $\neq 0$<br>$=0$ | $-1$<br>None | 3<br>5 |
| 3 | $B$ | Any | $+1$ | 4 |
| 4 | $B$ | Any | $+1$ | 2 |
| 5 | $B$ | $\neq 0$<br>$=0$ | $-1$<br>None | 6<br>1 |
| 6 | $A$ | Any | $+1$ | 5 |

FIG. 5

$\bar{B}=2$. At this point we are led on to instruction 5 and we must follow the instructions 6, 5, 6. This has the effect of transferring the contents of $B$ into $A$ so we have $\bar{A}=2$, $\bar{B}=0$. Instruction 5 now leads us back to instruction 1, and so to a halt, with answer $\bar{A}=2=2^1$.

Fig. 6 shows the successive configurations for the case $n=2$; the next instruction to be obeyed is shown at the bottom with the current contents of the three registers ('–' for 'empty') above it. By following this through the reader should convince himself that the effect of the repeated cycle of instruction (2, 3, 4) is to double the contents of $A$ and place it in $B$, and the effect of the repeated cycle (5, 6) is to transfer this number back to $A$. Hence each time a bead is removed from $C$ the total effect is to double the number in $A$. Thus the given programme does indeed compute $2^n$, however large $n$ may be.

A number of remarks about this process are in order.

(a) We have worked in the 'scale of one' instead of in the decimal scale. That is, a number is represented by the same number of beads, instead of using a units register, a tens register, and so on. Our method is hopelessly impractical—it is very extravagant in both space and time; but conceptually it is very simple.

(b) The table of instructions breaks down the computation into the simplest possible steps. It might be thought that this is only possible for rather simple mathematical operations like addition, multiplication, and exponentiation. But this is not the case. Any function of whole numbers which can be computed by an electronic computer, however sophisticated, can also be computed on a three-wire abacus using only instructions like the ones we have used. The advantages of sophistication are pragmatic—saving of time and money and increase of reliability. (We have of course supposed that the operator of our abacus does not make mistakes.)

(c) Our example illustrates the computation of a function. But we might equally well have considered a process of decision—for

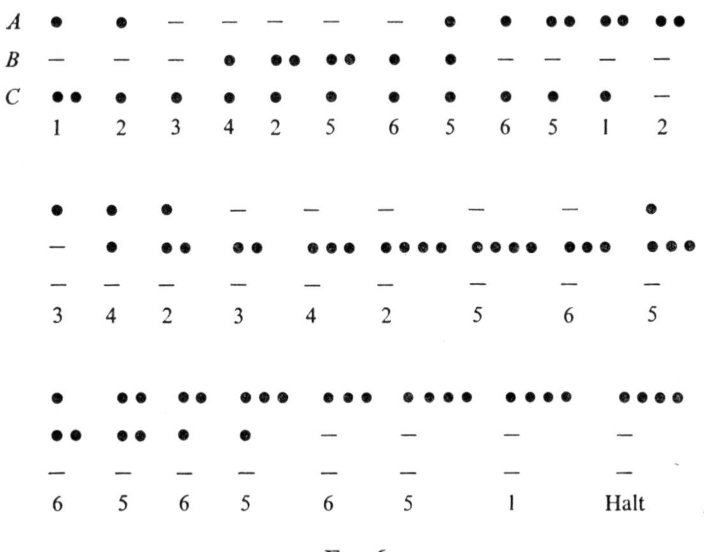


FIG. 6

example, is $n$ a prime number? This can be reduced to a function $f$ by setting, say, $f(n)=0$ if $n$ has the property, $f(n)=1$ if not.

(d) Our example is purely numerical, and it might be thought that quite different ideas would be required in non-numerical (e.g. linguistic) contents. This is not so, as can be seen in two ways. First, it is possible to code strings of symbols by numbers (a process often referred to as 'Gödel-numbering') in such a way that simple symbolic operations correspond to relatively simple numerical functions. Secondly, it is not hard to modify the idea of the abacus so as to cope with symbols. Each register will contain a string of symbols. The basic operations will be: (i) deciding whether the last symbol in a string is a particular symbol (to be named in the instruction) or not; (ii) adding a named symbol to the string; (iii) erasing the last symbol.

(e) The reader who wishes to pursue these ideas further is recommended to consult Minsky's book,[8] where justifications for the assertions made in the above remarks will be found. An account of the application of these ideas to abstract linguistics will be found in Hopcroft and Ullman.[9]

To sum up, an operation or decision process is computable if a fixed finite table of instructions can be drawn up for performing it in a finite, but not fixed, sequence of steps. The operations and decisions which occur in the instructions must be of a very elementary kind, so that it is intuitively obvious that they are computable. The analysis of the notion of computability which led to this characterization is due to A. M. Turing. What is remarkable, and what makes his work a paradigm of philosophical analysis, is that the above characterization does not depend on the details. The instructions may apply to an abacus, or to a multidimensional array of symbols, and the permitted operations and decisions can be chosen from a wide variety of possibilities; the extent of the concept remains unaltered. Even analyses of different, though cognate, notions such as 'effectively calculable', 'rule-governed', 'algorithmic' have led to equivalent characterizations. There can be no doubt that the concept is an important one. It is a presupposition for the philosophy of mathematics that a human being can *in principle* perform any computable process; abstracting from the practical limitations of time and space, we believe that he can follow any table of instructions of the kind considered. This raises an interesting point. Chomsky, more particularly in his controversies with Skinner, has distinguished between *performance* (such as reciting from memory, or threading a maze) and *competence* (such as being able to speak grammatically or being able to do arithmetic). It is natural to consider the ability to compute $2^n$ as a competence; on the other hand, to carry out one of the instructions in the table should surely count as a performance—it seems wholly reasonable to suppose that Professor Skinner could train his pigeons to slide beads and to distinguish whether there were any beads on the right or not. Thus one may say that Turing's analysis reduces the competence to compute to the ability to run through a sequence of performances. Since the length of the sequence depends on the argument $n$, we cannot say that competence is reduced to performance. (Boredom and lack of motivation would supervene to prevent a pigeon or rat carrying out the computation for, say, $n>4$.) But in this case a bridge between them is provided. We shall return to the discussion of competence later.

How is the notion of computability to be applied to abstract structures? First, to make sense of the notion, some structure must be given in advance—the notion of '$+1$' for numbers, or of adding a symbol to a string of symbols. One cannot do much computing with totally colourless individuals. Secondly, if the domain of individuals is infinite, then some properties and relations will not be computable. Consider, for example a question of the form: do all numbers $m$ bear the relation $R$ to the number $n$? In general this question can only be answered for given $n$ by an *infinite* series of trials corresponding to $m=0, 1, 2, \ldots$, and so we cannot expect a computable solution (though of course for particular $R$ there may be short cuts). Recently (1969) Matiasevitch, a young Russian mathematician, showed that there is no way of computing the solution to the 'Diophantine problem'. More precisely, there is an algebraic equation of the fourth degree in a not very large number of unknowns with integral coefficients such that there is no computable method for deciding for which values of the coefficients does the equation have an integral solution (i.e. a solution in whole numbers).

Some mathematicians have proposed that, roughly speaking, mathematics should only be concerned with computable structures since infinitistic processes which cannot, even in principle, be carried out are totally unreal. But the Platonist, infinitistic view of mathematics is now so much a part of the mathematical imagination and has produced such powerful and beautiful theorems, that the theory of computable structures appears to most mathematicians as a poor and shabbily dressed relation. But of course it is always of interest to know whether some infinitistically described process is or is not computable.

If we apply the notion of computability to languages, the obvious question is: is there a finite set of grammatical rules, and a finite lexicon, from which we can compute whether or not a given string of symbols (letters, spaces, and punctuation marks) is a correctly formed sentence? The structural linguists (in particular Chomsky) have certainly shown that the idiosyncrasies of, say, ordinary English are more often governed by syntactic rules than at first sight appears. But the question they have been primarily interested in is a slightly but significantly different one: not can one *decide* (like someone marking Latin sentences) if a sentence is correct, but is there a method for *generating* all correct sentences. We can translate this into our terms as follows. Suppose the table of instructions is not deterministic but allows for free choices (e.g. of a particular noun) at certain points. We can incorporate this idea as follows. In place of the argument $n$, we are given a list $s$ of those choices which are to be made when choice is called for. Then the table of instructions plus the list $s$ do determine the complete process and its final output (the generated sentence). This process is entirely analogous to the generation of the consequences of a given set of axioms mentioned on p. 138. And an analogue of Church's theorem holds: there is no computable process for deciding whether or not a given sentence can be generated from a given table of instructions. (For, checking that the proposed sentence is *not* so generated may require an *infinite* search through all possible lists $s$ of choices.) One of the ideals of structural linguistics is to provide rules of generation for any given language; this is thus less ambitious than seeking to provide rules for checking the correctness of proposed sentences.

At this point it is necessary to consider a philosophic objection. There are, in fact, upper bounds imposed on the length of a sentence by considerations of time (say, the life span of a man) and space (say, the surface of the earth). But this means there is only a finite number of possible sentences. Then the ideas and distinctions collapse: we can simply list once and for all the correct sentences of any language. A similar difficulty arises in theories of probability, where the definition of randomness (e.g. of the tosses of a coin) may be made in terms of infinite sequences, or of finite sequences of *unbounded* length. But just as the notion of computability is invariant under changes in the definition of 'elementary instruction', so is the *order of magnitude* of the length of a table of instructions invariant under *reasonable* changes in the type of instruction used. To say that a set of sentences each of length less than $N$ can be generated by some process is to say nothing at all; but to say that they can be generated by a table of instructions the order of magnitude of whose length is much less than $N$ is to say something highly significant. In this way the distinctions between lawless, generable, and computably checkable can be made sense of, even when they are applied to strings of symbols of *bounded* length.

We have been discussing linguistics in a very general and abstract way. At this level the only conclusion about human thought processes which has emerged so far is that human beings are capable of behaving like computers; that they can carry out a programme of instructions indefinitely, the only limitations being practical ones. But both our own experience and linguistic studies tell us that our competence goes much beyond this. In the first place we learn many of the rules of syntax by example, not by explicit instruction. In the second place we seem to be able to apply the rules without being conscious of what the rules are. One often can say that a particular sentence is ungrammatical without being able to name the rules which it violates. Chomsky has argued that these facts show that there is an *innate* generalized language-learning ability. It is as if certain *forms* of programme were built in; then exposure to a particular language results, gradually, in the specifying of various parameters until eventually the forms of programme have become actual programmes. I have the impression that although many details of the learning process for particular languages are known, yet we are still very far from any picture of the general process. Progress here could be very exciting; it might, for example, show why some kinds of mathematical structure seem more natural, more sympathetic, than others.

## NOTES

1. J.-M. Benoist, 'Structuralism', *Cambridge Review*, xciii, No. 2204 (22 Oct. 1971).
2. Iris Murdoch, *A Severed Head* (Chatto & Windus, London, 1961).
3. N. Bourbaki, *Éléments de mathématique*, i, *Théorie des ensembles* (Fascicule de Résultats) (Hermann et Cie., Paris, 1939).
4. J. Piaget, *Structuralism* (Routledge & Kegan Paul, London, 1971).
5. H. Weyl, *Symmetry* (Princeton University Press, Princeton, N.J., 1952).
6. C. Lévi-Strauss, *The Elementary Structures of Kinship* (Eyre and Spottiswoode, London, 1969).
7. A. S. Eddington, *The Philosophy of Physical Science* (Cambridge University Press, Cambridge, 1939).
8. M. L. Minsky, *Finite and Infinite Machines* (Prentice-Hall, Englewood Cliffs, N.J., 1964).
9. J. E. Hopcroft and J. D. Ullman, *Formal Languages and their Relation to Automata* (Addison-Wesley, Reading, Mass., 1969).

# *List of Contributors*

JONATHAN CULLER is Tutor in French and Fellow of Selwyn College, Cambridge; he is the author of the forthcoming *Structuralist Poetics* (Routledge and Kegan Paul, London, 1973).

UMBERTO ECO, a writer and journalist, teaches semiology at the University of Bologna and is the author of an extensive introduction to the subject, *La struttura assente* (Bompiani, Milan, 1968), soon to be published in English.

ROBIN GANDY is Reader in Mathematical Logic at Oxford University and a Fellow of Wolfson College. His chief work has been on the theory of recursive functions.

EDMUND LEACH is Provost of King's College, Cambridge, and Professor of Social Anthropology in the University. He has written, among other things, a study of the work of Lévi-Strauss (Fontana, London, 1970).

JOHN LYONS is Professor of Linguistics at the University of Edinburgh. He is the author of an *Introduction to Theoretical Linguistics* (Cambridge University Press, Cambridge, 1968), and of a study of Chomsky (Fontana, London, 1970).

JOHN MEPHAM teaches philosophy in the School of European Studies at the University of Sussex. He has specialized in epistemological problems, particularly in relation to the works of Marx and Freud.

TZVETAN TODOROV is an Attaché de Recherches at the French Centre National de la Recherche Scientifique. He is the author of a large number of original contributions to the field of literary theory, and an editor of the journal *Poétique*.

DAVID ROBEY teaches Italian at Oxford University and is a Fellow of Wolfson College.